they cannot expect to stop the forward line.
Rather, they seem to be *using* that momentum to
divide the mass of men into two. They are pushing
along a diagonal line that follows the direction of the
long pike held by the man at the back. This break in
the picture divides the right-hand side into two
triangles. And when I look closer, I notice that the
whole composition is made up of four triangles,
though alongside these principal divisions there are
all sorts of other direction indicators pointing various
ways."

Paul Claudel on *The Night Watch*
Dutch Painting, 1935

Watercolour copy
of *The Company
of Captain Frans
Banning Cocq*, known
as *The Night Watch*,
showing the painting in
its original state.

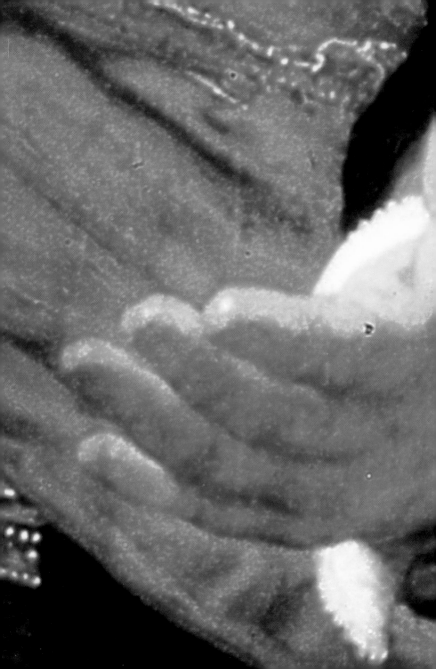

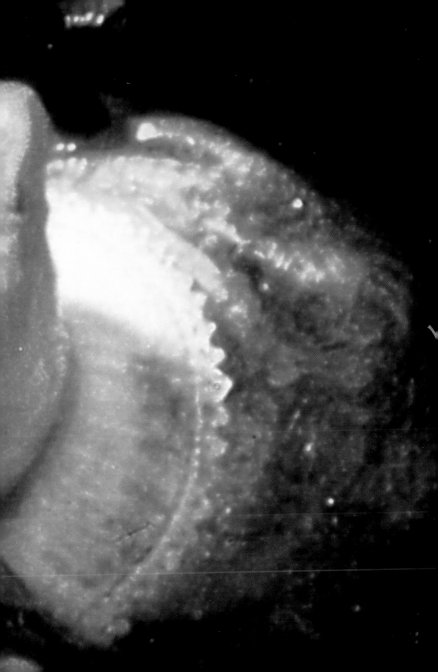

CONTENTS

1 APPRENTICESHIP AND AMBITION
13

2 REJOICING AND MOURNING
41

3 LONELINESS AND BANKRUPTCY
79

4 RETIREMENT AND DEATH
101

DOCUMENTS
129

Further Reading
168

List of Illustrations
168

Index
172

REMBRANDT
SUBSTANCE AND SHADOW

Pascal Bonafoux

THAMES AND HUDSON

Rembrandt van Rijn, son of Harmen Gerritszoon van Rijn and Neeltge Willemsdr van Suydtbroek, was born in Leiden on 15 July 1606. Johannes Orlers records the fact in a guide to the wonders of Leiden published in 1641. It is the only documentary evidence of the artist's date of birth: we have to accept an element of uncertainty in the story of his rise to fame and glory.

CHAPTER 1

APPRENTICESHIP AND AMBITION

The authenticity of *The Mill* (opposite), long attributed to Rembrandt, is now disputed. There is no doubt, however, about Rembrandt's etching of his father (left), dated 1630.

Harmen Gerritszoon – son of Gerrit, abbreviated to Gerritsz – van Rijn married Cornelia Willemsdochter – daughter of Willem, or Willemsdr – on 8 October 1589. Her nickname Neeltge – or Neeltgen – reveals her to be a baker's daughter. Harmen Gerritsz was a miller. He took the name van Rijn from the windmill he owned in the north of the town near the Wittepoort. It was in the Weddesteeg, a small street on the embankment of the Oude Rijn, or Old Rhine.

Another branch of the Rhine, the Nieuwe Rijn, forks upriver of the town and flows to the south of it. Between the two arms of the river lies a network of canals on which Leiden was built. The town numbered some forty thousand inhabitants at the beginning of the 16th century. It had made a successful recovery after the depredations of the 1574 siege and, in addition to its industries, boasted a university renowned throughout Europe.

Rembrandt's mother was a frequent and revered model in his Leiden days. This etching dated 1631 shows her dignified and pensive.

The van Rijn family has had connections with Leiden for nearly a century

In 1513 a van Rijn or Vande Rijn was a miller in the town. It is possible that Rembrandt owed his Christian name to his maternal great-grandmother, Reijmptje Cornelisdr van Blanchem. Reijmptje is not unlike Rembrandt, and spelling was not then standardized. A name suggesting a connection with the van Blanchems, an old and prominent family, may well have seemed opportune.

Leiden, founded in the 9th century, was historically called Lugdunum Batavorum. This plan (opposite) is of the town in 1574 at the end of the Spanish siege. The detail (below) of an engraving by Pieter Bast shows the skyline of Leiden and the flatness of the surrounding landscape in 1601.

Harmen Gerritsz converted to Calvinism, as had Reijmptje in his wife's family. Rembrandt's mother remained a Catholic. Rembrandt was her eighth child. The eldest was named Gerrit after his paternal grandfather. Like his father he was a miller. The second son, Adriaen, was a shoemaker. Two daughters came next but both died young. Rembrandt knew only one of his older sisters, whose name was Machteld. Closest to him were his older brothers Cornelis and Willem, both of whom had been born before the turn of the century. After Rembrandt, his mother gave birth to yet another daughter, Lijsbeth.

The van Rijn family was large, as families had to be to survive. Epidemics, disease and war all took their toll. The family was also comfortably off. It is not known whether, when the dikes broke, their mill was requisitioned to pump away the waters flooding the countryside. Harmen would not in any case have hesitated to give what help he could. War, fires in the towns and the ravages of the North Sea had taught the Dutch solidarity.

Fire and water: constant and terrible enemies

Holland had to defend herself against the sea as she had to defend herself against Spain. In 1606 no truce or treaty had been agreed. And although the Spanish were one day to retreat, the sea remained a permanent threat. Each year from November to February water seeped in, flooding the country as far as the eye could see. The dikes needed constant reinforcement. Indeed more men in the country worked for the *dykgrave* keeping them in repair than were engaged in tilling the soil. At long intervals numbered posts marked out sections of the dikes, which the villages along the coast were responsible for keeping under surveillance. These walls of earth, ceaselessly battered and eroded by the sea, were the only protection of a country described by a French traveller as 'scarcely fit for habitation'.

The brick house inhabited by Harmen Gerritsz van Rijn on the Weddesteeg, almost facing his mill, was

This detail of an early 17th-century map of Leiden shows the Wittepoort district in which the van Rijn family lived. Their house stood close to the mill, in a little street parallel to the quay of the Old Rhine.

A breach in the dike is portrayed in the detail (opposite) of *The St Elizabeth's Day Flood with Dordrecht in the Background*, an oil painting by a late 15th-century artist known only as the Master of the St Elizabeth Panels. As the waters gush in through the break, men pile their families, livestock and provisions into boats to escape the flood.

exactly like the other buildings lining the quayside. Freestone was a luxury building material, generally used by prosperous burghers and in public buildings. Each year, in common with his neighbours, Harmen Gerritsz van Rijn would display on his doorstep the buckets and ladders that the town authorities required every citizen to keep in readiness in case of fire. In Leiden, as in all towns in Holland, tar and pitch were used to light the streets and canals. The inevitable fire risk was aggravated by the fact that many houses were built of wood. The townspeople needed to be extremely vigilant.

The picture collectors of the United Provinces had a taste for scenes of daily life, such as *Recreation on the Ice* by Hendrick Avercamp (above), *The Meal* by Jan Steen (right) and the etching of *The Skater* by Rembrandt (below).

Pastimes and prayers

No sooner did winter freeze the canals than the van Rijns took to their skates, as did everyone else – magistrates, preachers, tradesmen.... Everybody dressed in the same coarse, dark cloth. They played games on the ice with clubs and balls.

The van Rijn family were not puritans who disapproved of the celebration of feast days. They went out with the throng to enjoy themselves, jostling with the best of them. Fiddlers scraped tunes in front of stalls. Tambourines and flageolets were played. There were roars of laughter at the tricks of the buffoons. And when the fun was over there were everyday amusements: dice, or the game of 'goose' using counters on a board. Preachers condemned the playing of cards, but they were in use everywhere, as popular in private houses as in the streets and taverns.

There was time for prayer too. Not a day went by without readings from the Holy Writ. Not a meal went by without the saying of grace. A blessing accompanied even the most frugal of repasts, *hoosepot*, a dish of boiled meat and vegetables cooked once a week and reheated daily.

1609. The war ends at last

In the name of Spain, Albert the Pious, Archduke of Austria and Governor of the Spanish Netherlands, made a Twelve Year Truce with the seven provinces which had adopted the Reformation, and was represented by Maurice of Nassau. The United Provinces was free.

In 1616 Adriaen Pietersz van de Venne painted an allegory of the Twelve Year Truce of 1609 (above). The couple advancing in the middle of the picture symbolize the United Provinces, recognized and liberated at last, while Discord and Envy have to take refuge behind a tree.

Deputies from each of the seven provinces made up the government, which had its headquarters at The Hague. It was headed by the Stadholder, a military leader whose function was to adjudicate more than to issue orders. A national figurehead, he had no fiscal or legislative power. The real authority in the United Provinces, the property-owning middle classes, was broadly held together by an abiding loyalty to the family of Orange. No one was exempt from tax. Money was there to mark differentials between men.

OOSTINDIS HVYS.
La Maison des Indes Orientales

S. Webbere fecit

Wealth from the East

In 1609 it was through the Dutch East India Company, founded seven years earlier, that fortunes were made and lost. Now everyone could aspire to a share of the action. That year the company appointed a governor for overseas territories. It drew together all the resources of the Netherlands, owned boats, quays, warehouses, shops, depots. It had a general staff running an army of several thousand men and a sizeable navy of vessels.

Around 1385 a fisherman from Zealand had struck upon a way of preserving the herring catch by packing the fish with salt into a barrel. This discovery had brought the beginnings of prosperity to the ports of the Zuiderzee. On the coasts of Friesland, Holland and Zealand, fishermen had to survive on cod, whiting and sole. It became clear to all that the Dutch East India Company held greater promises of riches than the herring barrel.

This plate of Delft china, its blue decoration based on the engravings of Adolf van der Laan, illustrates the packing of herrings into barrels. The use of salt to preserve herrings brought prosperity to the ports of the Zuiderzee.

A prosperous and puritanical bourgeoisie

The year 1609 again. The postal routes of Europe had for years been channelling financial information into Amsterdam. Now the bank of exchange was founded, confirming the city's status as a money market.

Dominated by the port, the church and the tavern, the citizens of Holland dreamt above all of the fortunes awaiting them in the East. They had two great preoccupations: their austere Calvinist faith, and their enthusiasm for overseas trade. Whereas the leaders were obsessed by wealth and status. This was the changed world into which Rembrandt was born, the world which he was to paint. No longer were the artist's sitters the regents and regentesses whose pride, portrayed by Frans Hals (who was born some twenty-five years before Rembrandt), was barely veiled by a hint of reserve.

With its ornamented gables and innumerable windows, the splendid front of East India Company House, seen in this 17th-century engraving (left), symbolized the newfound status conferred on the United Provinces by foreign trade.

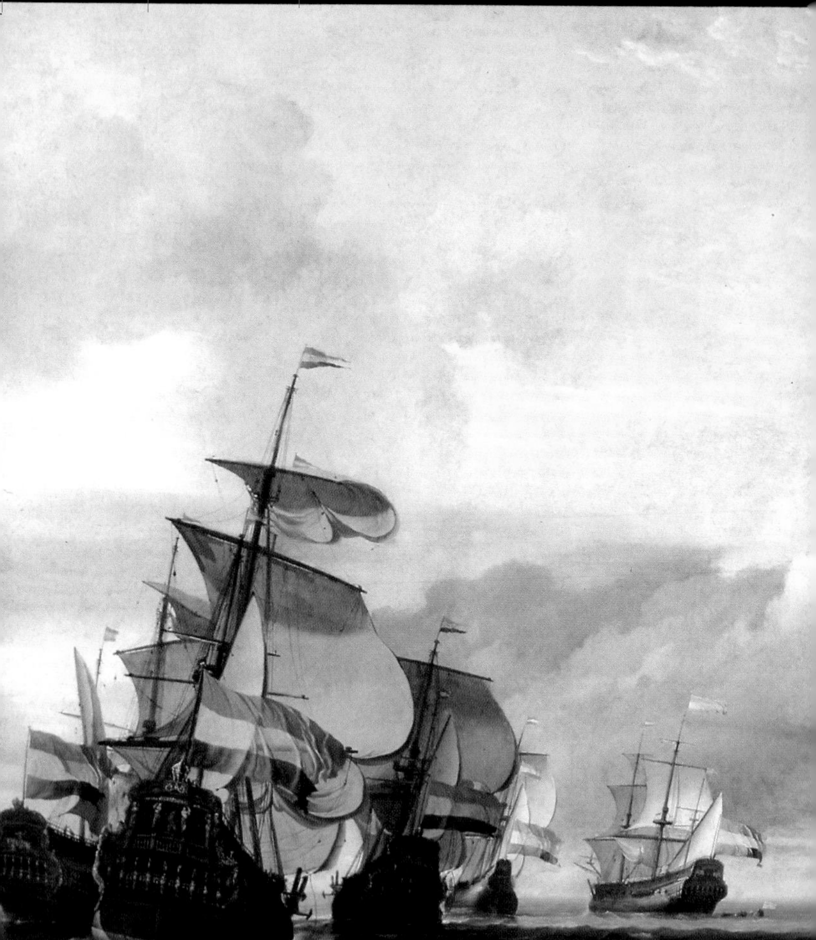

The sailors of Northern Holland, then at war with Spain, made a series of expeditions between 1595 and 1600 on which they set up warehouses, notably on the shores of the Indian Ocean. In 1614, at the other end of the world, they founded New Amsterdam by the mouth of the Hudson River – later, when it ceased to be a Dutch colony, to become New York. Lured by the promise of huge profits in the spice trade, ships set out in increasing numbers, vying with each other for markets and custom. In 1602 the myriad companies involved joined together to form the all-powerful Dutch East India Company. This painting of the *The Dutch Fleet of the East India Company* by Ludolf Backhuysen was directly commissioned by the company to commemorate its achievements. The majority of the vessels portrayed, three-masted ships with multiple decks and double forecastles, were of some 600 to 1000 tonnes (an average size, equally suited to both transport and piracy).

The men and women featured in the comparably serene light of Jan Vermeer (born some twenty-five years after Rembrandt) were characterized by a delicacy and polish akin to the elegance of the French.

In 1613 Rembrandt starts at the Latin school

There he learned to read and write, in Latin and in Dutch. He learned to read, and reread, the Bible. And he must indeed have learned. He entered the university of Leiden at the age of fourteen, which would not have been possible had he followed in the footsteps of his elder brothers, who went to work with their father at a very early age.

In 1675, six years after Rembrandt's death, his biographer Joachim von Sandrart claimed that he had scarcely been able to read Dutch and that 'books could hardly have been of great help to him' in studying the ancients and the theory of art. This seems unlikely: the university of Leiden would hardly have admitted a student who could not read. On 20 May 1620, between the names of a Nicolaus and a Gerardus, the university register reads: 'Rembrandus hermanni Leydensis studios litterarum annor 14 apud parentes' (RHL, student of letters, 14 years old, living with his parents).

The university at which Rembrandt enrolled to study the humanities was founded by the state

It had colleges, a library, and lodgings for the students, who were drawn from all over Europe. The teachers were sold accommodation by the municipality in the Grand Béguinage. The university was not bound by any medieval tradition and the subjects studied included the sciences, oriental languages, Greek, Latin, astrology, anatomy and botany, a botanical garden having been created in Leiden in 1587 by Clusius. As an aid to scientific study, the town and its surroundings had been equipped with thermometers, telescopes, barometers.

Rembrandt spent only a few months at university. It was enough nevertheless to exempt him from service in the civil guard and the obligation to pay tax on wine

The painter Frans Hals belonged to a generation for whom verve was more important than sobriety. This is apparent in his portrait of *Paulus van Beresteyn*, a judge in Haarlem (detail below).

The frontispiece of the Statenbijbel (above), the only version of the Bible recognized by the Calvinist United Provinces. It was published in 1637 in Leiden, a notable printing centre.

THECÆ LUGDUNO-BATAVÆ CUM PULPITIS ET ARCIS VERA IXNOGRAPH

Founded in 1575, renowned throughout Europe, the university of Leiden was the oldest in Holland. The library, shown in this engraving by Jacob van Swanenburgh (left), was used for study and as a meeting-place. It housed the earliest printed works of science and philosophy. Van Swanenburgh also engraved the anatomy theatre of the university of Leiden (below). Already in the early 1600s medical men and interested minds were attending anatomy lessons given by noted professors.

and beer, in addition to a number of other privileges. He was not interested in Latin or the study of the 'Statenbijbel' (State Bible) prescribed by the Great Synod of Dordrecht in 1618 and 1619 and printed by government order.

In 1641 Johannes Orlers recorded the anxieties of Rembrandt's parents about his education: 'As he showed neither taste nor aptitude in this field, his natural bent tending solely to painting and drawing, they found themselves obliged to withdraw their son from the school and decided to place him with a painter so that he could learn the foundations and principles of art. They thus sent him

VERA ANATOMIÆ LUGDUNO-BATAVÆ, CUM SCELETIS ET RELIQVIS QVÆ IBI EXTANT DELINEATIO

to the master Jacob Isaacsz van Swanenburgh, to whom it fell to instruct and mould him.'

Van Swanenburgh is a mediocre painter

Whether one considers his portraits, his architectural views or, for what they are worth, his fantasies, Rembrandt's first master, who worked in the manner of Hieronymus Bosch, was not an outstanding artist. He owed his reputation to a sojourn in Italy, from which he had returned to Leiden in 1617, at the age of forty-six, with a Neapolitan wife, Margherita Cordona.

As in any studio, pupils were taught to pounce wood, prepare a canvas and grind colours. The apprentice artist had to start by learning the basic procedures. Rembrandt studied the elementary principles of drawing, anatomy and perspective. In three years he had learnt all that van Swanenburgh was able to teach him.

In 1641, the year Johannes Orlers published his guide to Leiden, Rembrandt was still remembered as an excellent student: 'He made so much progress that the professionals were left astonished. It was clear that he would one day become an outstanding painter. His father thought the time had come to send him to the highly esteemed painter Pieter Pieterszoon Lastman, who lived in Amsterdam, that he might be given better and more intensive instruction.'

Pieter Lastman is a more important influence than van Swanenburgh

Like van Swanenburgh, Lastman had spent several years in Italy. He had met Adam Elsheimer in Rome and might also have come across Caravaggio there. In any case he had seen and remembered his work. Lastman painted mythological and biblical subjects. He had no interest

Rembrandt was only twenty in 1626 when he painted *The Angel and the Prophet Balaam* or *Balaam and the Ass* (below), signing it with the monogram RL: L stood for his birthplace, Leiden. His source was clearly Pieter Lastman's painting of the same subject (opposite below), which he would have seen in his master's studio in Amsterdam. He handled his model freely: while the gestures of the prophet on his mount are similar, Rembrandt invests the virtually static pose of Lastman's angel with a flowing sense of movement accentuated by the sweep of the draped clothes.

in scenes of everyday life such as taverns, village fairs or guild and corporation banquets; nor did he paint landscapes or still-lifes.

Lastman owed his reputation to his history painting. He was forty-one and Rembrandt eighteen when they worked together. In six months Rembrandt mastered Lastman's subject matter and the art of composition. This brief period had a decisive influence on him.

This *Entombment* by Lastman, painted following his return to Holland, evokes the work of Caravaggio in its use of light. While he had adopted chiaroscuro, Lastman nonetheless did not rival Rembrandt in his composition and failed to achieve a truly dramatic effect.

Rembrandt returns to Leiden confident of his abilities

It was a short journey of some forty kilometres, usually undertaken in a flat-bottomed barge towed along the

canal. In Leiden Rembrandt set up his own studio, probably in his father's house on the Weddesteeg. He worked with another painter, Jan Lievens, barely a year younger than himself. Like Rembrandt, Lievens was from Leiden and had been one of Lastman's pupils in Amsterdam. At the age of eight, when Rembrandt was at the Latin school, Lievens started his apprenticeship with a Leiden painter, Joris van Schooten. (Might Rembrandt too have passed through his studio?) He then moved to Lastman's studio in Amsterdam. By the time he was eighteen Lievens had had many years experience. Now the two artists had only to paint. To make their name. And to sell.

In Holland a painter is just another citizen

Neither church nor state commissioned works of art. Chapels were bare of paintings and altarpieces. And the funds at the disposal of the Stadholder were by no means princely. An artist thus had to obtain his commissions from his fellow citizens. These were men constantly aware of the Bible and of their own dignity. They had no desire to be patrons, they were simply clients whose requirements the artist had to meet.

Jan Lievens and Rembrandt worked together in their studio. As Rembrandt signed himself RL, Lievens used the monogram IL in his *Self-portrait, c.* 1635 (detail below). The L could have referred to his name or his birthplace.

The sea, sky, storm clouds and mists were the natural setting of life in Holland. Below: Salomon van Ruysdael's *Ferry* (detail).

In particular they expected that a painting should reflect their sobriety and their ambition. They wanted to recognize themselves, the spirit that drove them, in a picture, and to be recognized.

The 'miller's son' is talked about

In 1628 Aernout van Buchell, a jurist and broker from Utrecht, visited Leiden and remarked in his *Res pictoriae* that a 'miller's son' there was very highly

esteemed, adding in Latin 'sed ante tempus' (but prematurely). What painting or paintings might van Buchell have seen to prompt this remark? Perhaps *The Stoning of St Stephen*, oil on wood signed and dated 'Rf 1625', and Rembrandt's earliest known work; though it may already have left the artist's studio.

This painting of *The Cathedral of St Bavo in Haarlem* (detail above) shows an austere interior, bare of frescos and paintings. It is by Pieter Jansz Saenredam.

In *The Stoning of St Stephen* (above left) Rembrandt boldly tackles a genre esteemed throughout Europe. Painting meant the portrayal of history, both sacred and profane. The serene face of the saint amongst the men about to stone him is given Rembrandt's features.

Other candidates – though again these might have been sold by 1628 – would have been *David Presenting the Head of Goliath to Saul, Anna Accused by Tobit of Stealing the Kid*, signed and dated 'RH 1626', and *Christ Driving the Moneychangers from the Temple*; also *The Music Party*, a delightful scene of provincial life in which the artist's brothers and sisters were used as models. Further paintings that could have fuelled Rembrandt's rising reputation are *St Paul in Prison, Two Scholars Disputing, The Flight into Egypt*, and *Samson and Delilah*, painted in 1627. Or was it *The Moneychanger* that van Buchell saw? Or *St Peter's Denial of Christ*?

Perhaps Rembrandt had hung his portrait of his father on his studio wall: an old man in a dark cap, head bent forward, white beard partly plunged in shadow; or one of his self-portraits, in which the glints in his hair were achieved by exposing the wood underneath (probably by scratching the paint with the handle of the paintbrush).

Rembrandt's *Old Man with a White Beard*, painted in 1626, was probably his father. The face would have fitted in his painting of *Christ Driving the Moneychangers from the Temple* (right).

Several titles have been given to Rembrandt's painting on wood (left), of 1626: *The Clemency of Titus, The Condemnation of the Son of Manlius Torquatus, The Judgment of Brutus, The Consul Cerialis and the German Legions*. At the age of twenty he was set to prove his mastery of history painting and powers of invention. The face partly obscured by the upraised sceptre is his own.

The subject of this picture, *Anna Accused by Tobit of Stealing the Kid*, was taken by Rembrandt from the Bible (Tobit II, 11–4). It is a painting dating from 1626. Tobit, blinded by the hot droppings of sparrows, heard the bleating of an animal brought home by his wife. He called to her and said, 'Where does this creature come from? Suppose it has been stolen! Quick, let the owners have it back; we have no right to eat

stolen goods.' She said, 'No, it was a present given me over and above my wages.' He did not believe her, and told her to give it back to the owners. Then she answered, 'What about your own alms? What about your own good works? Everyone knows what return you have had for them.' Tobit sighed and wept and began a prayer of lamentation.

Rembrandt might also have shown van Buchell his self-portrait of *The Artist in his Studio*, standing before the easel, a palette, a bunch of paintbrushes and a cane gripped in his left hand. This is the portrait of his ambition. The wooden panel resting horizontally on the easel corresponds in shape and size to Rembrandt's paintings of biblical subjects. And once an artist had mastered these....

In 1626 Rembrandt begins to etch the biblical scenes he has already painted

He etched *The Circumcision* and *The Rest on the Flight into Egypt* that year and *The Flight into Egypt* a year later. Again and again he etched his mother's face and beggars in rags. Was this because wrinkles, stains and tattered edges could readily be rendered in line and shadow?

In 1678 Samuel van Hoogstraten recorded in his *Introduction to the Elevated School of Painting* a precept Rembrandt held up to his pupils: 'Make it a rule consciously to practise what you already know; you will then discover that which escapes you and what you wish to learn.'

Did Rembrandt himself apply this principle? He was always eager to learn more. Thus he set out to master the new technique of etching. No doubt he had seen the

Rembrandt did many drawings and etchings of the beggars of Leiden over the years, among them the *Beggar in High Cap, Leaning on a Stick* (left) of 1629. His etching needle found inspiration in torn clothes and lined faces. The portrait of his mother's head (far left) is from 1628.

The painter gazing at the panel propped on the easel in full light is Rembrandt himself. Is he in this self-portrait of *The Artist in his Studio* contemplating a finished work or a rough sketch? He is not in working apparel but dressed as if to receive clients, implying a certain status. The scene was painted *c.* 1628.

etchings of Willem Pietersz Buytewech, Esaias van de Velde, Pieter Vinckboons and Hercules Seghers. No doubt he had begun to buy Jacques Callot's works. Rembrandt was convinced that acid offered greater possibilities as an etching tool than the burin. However, he had to learn to use different varnishes, control the depth of the biting of the acid, change the etching needles. This required endless practice. He devised a double needle and used it to etch the strands of his own hair.

Rembrandt was also influenced by engravings of other artists, such as Dürer. In *Beggar with a Crippled Hand, Leaning on a Stick* (above) he was clearly inspired by the work of Jacques Callot, an example being *Beggar with a Crutch* (left).

Rembrandt is not yet twenty. He works and experiments with unflagging energy

In the late 1620s Lievens was probably more highly regarded than Rembrandt. It was Lievens who, in about 1626, painted the portrait of Constantijn Huygens (detail left). The latter, some ten years older than the two young artists, was a useful connection. He had served as a diplomat at the embassy of the United Provinces in the Venetian Republic and afterwards at the embassy in London, where James I ennobled him. In 1625 he became private secretary to the Stadholder. Huygens translated Latin verse and the poetry of John Donne, studied law, astronomy and theology and conducted a correspondence with Descartes in three languages. He also kept a diary.

In approximately 1630 Huygens recorded that the 'miller's son', Rembrandt, and the 'embroiderer's son', Lievens, were already the equals of the most famous painters and would soon surpass them. He went on to draw the moral that the men's humble origins proved the vanity of those who claimed their noble blood conferred superiority.

Comparing the two painters to their teachers, Huygens expressed the opinion that they owed them nothing. 'If today they could see the work of their pupils, they would feel the same shame as the teachers of Virgil, Cicero and Archimedes.' Huygens also

Constantijn Huygens commissioned Jan Lievens to paint his portrait (detail top left) c. 1626. He wrote the first criticism of Rembrandt's work, remarking on his use of light and shade.

compared the two men to each other: Lievens was superior in invention, while Rembrandt showed greater judgment and more lively emotional expression. Taking the example of *Judas Returning the Thirty Pieces of Silver*, Huygens declared (see pp. 136–7) that the painting outdid everything that had been produced by antiquity and Italy: an adolescent, son of a Batavian miller, had here surpassed Protogenes, Apelles and Parrhasius.

Huygens was impressed by Rembrandt's *Judas Returning the Thirty Pieces of Silver* of 1629 (above). The drawing of two figures (far left) may have been a sketch for the painting.

How can you be a painter without going to Rome?

Huygens was astonished that the two young painters had spent no time in Italy. What 17th-century artist had not visited the country? Poussin, Rubens, Velazquez – the list was endless – had measured their strength in Rome and the city had continued to serve them as a reference point and to provide models. Neither Lievens nor Rembrandt had thought the journey necessary, for two reasons: because a good number of Italian masterpieces found their way to Holland and because they lacked the time. The second reason was doubtless the most cogent. Though their attitude surprised Huygens, it was no obstacle to their growing reputation. Robert Ker, the Earl of Ancrum, personal envoy of Charles I, visited the United Provinces. Among the works the Stadholder entrusted to him for the king of England were paintings by Lievens and Rembrandt.

First pupils, first sales

Gerrit Dou was the first student to attend Rembrandt's studio. He was then fourteen years old. Huygens' visits to the studio and the advent of pupils were both signs of Rembrandt's growing reputation. Every means of making himself known seemed worth pursuing.

Fifty years after Rembrandt's death the Dutch writer Arnold Houbraken gave the following convincing

In 1631, the year he left Leiden, Rembrandt painted *The Prophetess Anna.* Anna had recognized the Child Jesus as the Messiah when he was brought by his parents to the Temple. Did Rembrandt's mother, who posed for this painting, realize her son's genius?

account: 'Every now and then he would be visited by connoisseurs; eventually they recommended that he visit a certain gentleman in The Hague to show him and offer him a newly finished painting. Rembrandt carried the painting to The Hague on foot, and sold it for one hundred guilders. This brilliant beginning opened up the possibility of wealth to him, and his enthusiasm for work redoubled, earning him the admiration of all art-lovers; now, as the saying went, he had his hands full of work.'

On 23 April 1630 Harmen Gerritsz van Rijn died, aged sixty-two. Rembrandt's brothers took charge of the mill. Did the loss of his father mean that Rembrandt had to work harder and sell more? There is no evidence that this is the case. Fame was his spur. Leiden became constricting. Johannes Orlers recorded: 'The successful reception given to his works in Amsterdam in 1630, to which he was often invited to paint portraits and other pictures, led him to move there.'

In Leiden most of his portraits had been a preparation for his history paintings, members of his family generally serving as models. Rembrandt's mother thus posed for *The Prophetess Anna* and appears as the central figure in *The Presentation of Christ in the Temple*. These portraits were already powerfully expressive and transcended the limitations of what was seen to be a minor genre.

This portrait of *An Old Woman* or *Rembrandt's Mother* is by Gerrit Dou. He may have copied a now lost painting by his master. There was frequent overlapping in the work of master and pupils in the studio: to copy was not to 'fake', but a way of learning and contributing.

" If it gives us pleasure to see fruit grow in our orchards, do you not think it will give us as much pleasure to see vessels arrive here bringing an abundance of all the produce of India and all that is rare in Europe? What other country could one find in which all the luxuries of life and all the rarities one could desire are so easily available?"

René Descartes

CHAPTER 2

REJOICING AND MOURNING

In Jan van der Heyden's painting of *The Herrengracht in Amsterdam* (detail opposite) we see the houses of the well-to-do.

Rembrandt's etching of a *View of Amsterdam* shows the city's port, vessels, windmills, clock towers and warehouses.

René Descartes, in exile, described the 'luxuries' and 'rarities' of Amsterdam to his friend the writer Jean Louis Guez de Balzac and observed: 'Everyone is so engrossed in furthering his own interests that I could spend the whole of my life here without being noticed by a soul.'

Business was indeed thriving. The French writer François de Salignac de la Motte Fénelon later recounted that people came from all over the world to deal, buy and sell in Amsterdam, whose citizens were 'the most eminent merchants in the world'. So numerous were the vessels in the harbour that from a distance the masts looked to him like a forest. Three concentric canals, or *grachten*, had been dug in Amsterdam, determining the layout of the city. The Westerkerk was finished and façades of brick and stone were rising all along the quays. Building site, market-place, principal port of

The development of Rembrandt's signature reflects his growing ambition. From the simple initials of his early years, he moved to signing only his Christian name – as he also moved away from Leiden and his humble beginnings.

Holland, Amsterdam was a city packed with fascination. It had overtaken Antwerp in importance as a port.

The arrival from Leiden in 1631 of Casparus Barlaeus, Professor of Philosophy and Medicine, was followed by that of other illustrious men, marking the will to establish Amsterdam as a centre of creativity, research and discovery. A university was founded. In the words of the Dutch poet and dramatist Joos van den

The portrait of René Descartes (above left) is after Frans Hals. It testifies to the encounter of a great philosopher and a brilliant portraitist.

Vondel, it was Amsterdam that wore 'the crown of Europe', and 'here resided the soul of the state of Holland'.

Rembrandt establishes himself in Amsterdam

The young painter was soon signing his works simply 'Rembrandt', or occasionally still 'R. van Rijn'. In the past he had preferred 'RHL van Rijn' (R for Rembrandt, H for Harmensz, L for Leydensis) or the initials RHL. Now there was no need to go on using the name of his father, Harmen, who had died in 1630. And why mention a connection with Leiden when he had left it? The quick progression to signing 'Rembrandt' followed by 'f', 'fe' or 'ft', representing the Latin *fecit* (made), betrays

the extent of his ambition. He wanted to be known by his first name alone like the great Italian masters, Titian, Raphael, Michelangelo.... At the age of twenty-seven he saw himself as their equal.

An important commission: a group portrait of an anatomy lesson

For months Rembrandt had been making regular trips from Leiden to work on commissioned portraits. It was probably the Amsterdam art dealer Hendrick van Ulenborch, with whom he had formed a partnership for a thousand guilders (a contract dated 29 June 1631 bears witness), who procured his most prestigious commission. The dealer had only been operating in the city since 1627, having lived in Poland and Denmark.

The Amsterdam Exchange was built between 1608 and 1611. Dealing took place not in the building itself but in the courtyard, the arcades providing shelter when it rained. *The Courtyard of the Old Exchange, Amsterdam* (detail above), dated 1653, is by the Dutch painter Emanuel de Witte. This artist had recently moved to Amsterdam, where he concentrated on architectural paintings. The word bourse ('exchange') comes from the van der Burse family, whose house in Bruges was used for financial dealings.

"The spiral of a winding stair descending from the shadows, and the glimpse of a deserted gallery, imperceptibly give the viewer the impression that he is examining the interior of a strange shell inhabited by a little intellectual animal who has secreted the luminous substance. The idea of withdrawal into oneself, of depths, of a richness of understanding born within the individual self, are suggested by this composition which in some vague, but inexpressible way, has a spiritual content."

Paul Valéry
The Return from Holland. Descartes and Rembrandt, 1926

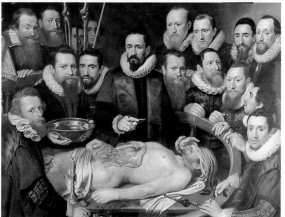

He handled works of art from all over Europe, particularly from Italy. Convinced of Rembrandt's talent, he guaranteed him board and lodging and also provided him with a studio in his own house. He encouraged Rembrandt to rank himself alongside the great masters.

The prestigious commission was to paint an anatomy lesson given in January 1632 by the forty-year-old Professor Nicolaas Pieterszoon Tulp using the corpse of a criminal sentenced to death. The painting was

The artistic tradition of anatomy lessons went back a hundred years. Typical were the anatomy lessons of Dr Sebastian Egbertsz by Thomas de Keyser (top left) and of Dr van der Meer by Pieter van Miereveld (below left), with rows of worthies.

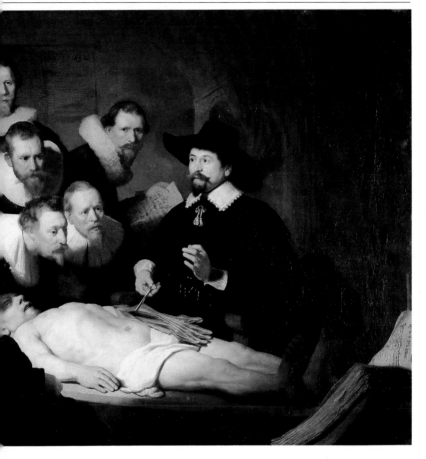

probably to mark the first anniversary of the lessons given by the professor in the anatomical theatre of the Anthoniesmarkt. The finished work was to hang in one of the guild halls. This place was significant for Rembrandt as only people of note frequented it, Tulp being one of them. A well-known surgeon, he had twice been elected burgomaster of the town and remained a magistrate. This was the man Rembrandt was commissioned to paint, in the company of others as illustrious as himself, though none was a surgeon.

In Rembrandt's *The Anatomy Lesson of Professor Tulp* the men round Tulp are not doctors. The list held by the man in the centre bears the names of government officials. But the fame the picture now immortalizes belongs to the artist.

Rembrandt knows his anatomy lesson will invite comparisons and be crucial to his career

If approved and admired, the work would lead to a brilliant future. What Rembrandt had to do was to astonish and yet to win acceptance, to startle the viewer, while respecting the solemnity of the occasion.

Group portraits had been current in Holland for over a century. *The Anatomy Lesson of Professor Tulp* thus had both to respect tradition and stand out from the rest.

The conventional group portrait presented its sitters in formal pose in an even light. Whether they were round a banqueting or council table, or in an anatomy theatre, made little difference to the manner in which they were portrayed. Their attitudes remained stiff, and they seemed virtually indifferent to the occasion. By contrast the men round Tulp seem to be genuinely attending an anatomy lesson. They bend over the corpse in silent concentration, examining the exposed tendons

There was a sculpted tulip on the front of the house of the *praefector anatomiae*, Professor Tulp (portrait below, detail). His name is Dutch for tulip and the flower something of a national emblem. Appointed magistrate in 1622 and twice elected burgomaster, Tulp was an established figure in Amsterdam society. Rembrandt probably studied the plates in *De humani corporis fabrica* by Andreas Vesalius, the celebrated Flemish anatomist and friend of Titian, when he painted this work.

of the dissected arm. Rembrandt was aware that the men posing for him wanted all who saw the portrait to appreciate their importance and learning. The dominant figure in the group is thus used, by the significant look in his eyes, to convey a sense of moment.

The painting astonishes Rembrandt's clients, while respecting their sensibilities; it wins him instant renown

On 26 July 1632 Rembrandt received a visit from a bailiff who had come to check that he was alive and well. The bailiff had been sent by men who had laid wagers on the health of celebrities in Amsterdam. Rembrandt was one of their number.

Now a young and famous painter, he met a cousin or niece of the colleague with whom he lived on the corner of Zwanenburgwal and Sint Anthoniesbreestraat. She came from Friesland, where her father had been burgomaster of Leeuwarden and a member of the tribunal. She had been born on 2 August 1612 and her name was Saskia. This young woman with rounded chin and full breasts was an orphan. Her father had died when she was twelve. She was also the youngest of her family – which did not preclude her having a dowry of forty thousand guilders. Unusually for a girl in those days, she knew how to read and write.

On 5 June 1633 Rembrandt and Saskia become engaged

Rembrandt drew Saskia's portrait shadowed by the brim of a flowery hat. Under the line of the edge of the table on which she rests her elbows, a smile on her lips and a flower in her hand, Rembrandt wrote: 'Portrait of my wife, when she was twenty-one years old, the third day after we were betrothed.' Like his father and mother, Saskia became Rembrandt's model.

A year to the day after their betrothal Rembrandt and Saskia's guardian, the preacher Jan Cornelisz Sylvius, went to the commissioners in Amsterdam to arrange the marriage. Rembrandt had still to obtain his mother's consent, a note of which was added later in the margin, having been registered before a notary in Leiden. The

couple left for Friesland. On 22 June 1634 Rembrandt and Saskia were married in the Reformed Church of Sint Annaparochie, the chief town of Het Bilt. A few weeks earlier, in the album of Burchard Grossmann, a German merchant staying with Hendrick van Ulenborch, Rembrandt had written: 'An upright man respects honour before wealth.' He could well afford such sentiments, given Saskia's dowry and the influx of commissions.

Rembrandt Harmensz van Rijn, son of a miller from Leiden, now had lawyers and an officer as his

Rembrandt's first portrait of Saskia, as his betrothed (above). Docile, almost resigned in her expression of good humour, did Saskia realize, as she sat for *Saskia Smiling with a Plumed Beret* (right), that she was embarking on a career as a model?

brothers-in-law. One of his sisters-in-law, Hiskje, had married the prosperous Gerrit van Loo. Marriage radically altered Rembrandt's social status: 'the miller's son' was a man of the past.

Rembrandt in love. Rich. Famous

He received a commission from the Stadholder himself. A year later he wrote to Constantijn Huygens, who had doubtless obtained it for him: 'My dear Sir and most gracious Mr Huygens, I hope your lordship will be so kind as to advise His Excellency that I am very diligently engaged in proficiently completing the three Passion pictures which His Excellency has personally commissioned me [to do]: an Entombment, a Resurrection, and an Ascension of Christ. These are companion pictures to Christ's Elevation [*The Raising*

The light in *The Raising of the Cross* (above left) falls diagonally along the line traced by the figures of Christ and the soldier raising the cross. Like *The Descent from the Cross* (detail above), this was one of five paintings commissioned from Rembrandt in 1634 by the Stadholder of the United Provinces, Frederick Henry. The common theme was the Passion of Christ.

of the Cross] and His Descent from the Cross. Of these above three, one has been completed, namely Christ's Ascension to Heaven, and the other two are more than half-finished. Please, Sir, let me know whether it would please His Excellency to have the finished piece first, or all three together, so that I may best serve His Excellency the Prince, according to his desires. As a token of my readiness to serve you with my favour, I cannot refrain from presenting to you, dear Sir, my latest work. I trust that you will most graciously accept it in addition to my greetings. I command your lordship and all of yours to God and health. Your obliging and affectionate servant, Rembrandt.'

Anxious to receive some payment in advance for what he had already done, he added the postscript: 'I reside next door to the pensionary Boereel on Niuwe [sic]

Because it is monochrome *The Entombment*, probably painted in 1639, is thought by some experts to be a sketch for one of Rembrandt's paintings for the Stadholder. The agreed fee for each was 600 guilders. The form of the five canvases supplied supports this hypothesis, the upper edge of each has the same arc.

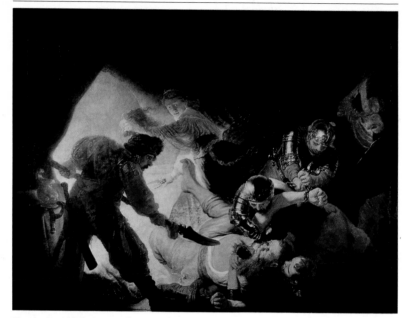

Doelstraat.' The Amstel Canal flowed past their house. Saskia and Rembrandt had thus spent some two years with van Ulenborch. Now they needed more space.

Master and pupils

Rembrandt took pupils. Among them were Ferdinand Bol, Govaert Flinck, Jacob Adriaensz Backer, Gerbrand van den Eekhout. Some of them had to be provided with a place to live. Painting, etching and the teaching of painting and etching required space. In 1635 he set up a studio in a vast old warehouse giving on to the Bloemgracht. In the same year Saskia became pregnant for the first time. Rumbartus was born and baptized in December, but lived only two months.

Rembrandt painted, drew and etched. He taught his pupils to measure the proportions of a body, to ink a copper plate, to grind colours. He made love to Saskia, drank beer and gin and frequented the auction rooms. Rembrandt wanted everything: to have everything, to understand everything.

Rembrandt gave *The Blinding of Samson* (above) to Constantijn Huygens to thank him for procuring commissions from the Stadholder. It is a violent scene which, in the harshness of its composition, brings Rembrandt close to a tradition of Italian art.

Whether by Rembrandt or one of his pupils, the drawing of *The Studio* (left) is vivid evidence of what went on there: the painter is at work with the model, one pupil is grinding colours, another sketching or reading.

The greedy Rembrandt

He studied works he would never see and sketched towns he would never visit. He copied Leonardo da Vinci's *Last Supper*, drew views of London, and Italian landscapes. He needed to dream dreams, as he needed to study his surroundings or to observe Saskia's pose with a child in arms.

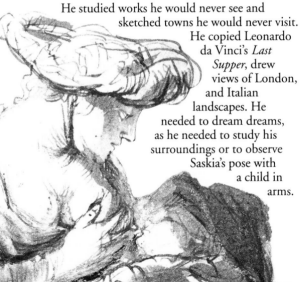

Rembrandt covered all manner of subjects in his studio, ranging from *The Pancake Woman* in the street (above) to a *Mother Nursing her Child* (left), in this case drawn by one of his pupils, Ferdinand Bol.

Saskia, model of love

This painting by Rembrandt has been taken variously to be *Artemisia Receiving the Ashes of Mausolus* or *Sophonisba Receiving the Poisoned Cup*. In either case the subject of the painting touches on marital fidelity and Saskia, present in so many of Rembrandt's fantasies, served as the model. She is also featured in Rembrandt's *Self-portrait with Saskia* (below) of 1636.

Goddess and woman

Rembrandt did not confine himself to straightforward portraits of Saskia. She appeared in many guises in his paintings. In *Saskia as Flora* (far left) she is the goddess of the Italian countryside. Possibly someone had mentioned to Rembrandt that prostitutes in Rome invoked the protection of Flora, but the portrait's sensuality in any case speaks for itself. The artist gives his Roman goddess a Dutch flavour by slipping a tulip into her floral wreath. In the *Portrait of Saskia van Ulenborch* (detail left) Rembrandt presents her as formidably elegant, her hat betraying an awareness of French fashions. Both paintings date from 1634.

As he needed to scrutinize the heavy trudge of a couple of peasants or a woman making pancakes.

Wearying of the unrelieved severity of his commissioned portraits – models attired in black set off by lace collars or ruffs – he decked old men out in turbans, robes and weapons and used them as models.

Rembrandt's *Self-portrait with Saskia* (1636) was his reply to those detractors who accused him of wasting his wife's dowry. He raises his glass to them.

He bought scimitars, brocades and silks for these portraits, and engravings and canvases to copy. Saskia's family grew worried by his extravagance and accused Rembrandt of squandering his wife's dowry. Rembrandt retorted that he was rich and that was the end of it. Who could deny it?

The impatient Rembrandt

Even the Stadholder owed him money, as he had no hesitation in reporting to Constantijn Huygens in a letter written 'in haste this 27 January 1639'. He told him that the tax collector Uytenbogaert had called while he was wrapping two works for the Stadholder and added: 'He mentioned that if it pleased His Highness, he was prepared to make payments to me from his office here. Therefore, may I ask you, my dear Sir, that the money which His Highness allows me for these two pieces be paid here as soon as possible, because I could use it well, particularly at the present time.' A few weeks passed. Rembrandt grew impatient: 'My dear Sir, I hesitate to trouble you with this letter, but I am doing so because of what Uytenbogaert, the tax collector, told me after I complained to him about the delay in my payment. Volbergen, the treasurer, denied that dues were claimed annually. Last Wednesday, Uytenbogaert, the collector, replied to this that Volbergen had thus far laid claim to these dues every six months,

Jan Uytenbogaert, the Receiver-General or *The Goldweigher.*

Rembrandt, a collector, owned a few Indian miniatures which inspired drawings such as *Two Men Standing in Oriental Dress.*

so that more than 4000 k. guilders had been deposited again at his office. And because of this true state of affairs, I beg you, kind Sir, to have my payment order prepared promptly, so that I will now finally receive my well-earned 1244 guilders.'

This sum was twice the 600 guilders Rembrandt had reluctantly agreed for each canvas – less than he might have hoped – plus 44 guilders to cover the cost of the ebony frame and the packing. Rembrandt again gave his address: 'I reside on the Binnen Amstel. The house is called the sugar bakery.' This shop, De Vier Suykerbrooden, where he had lived for several weeks, belonged to a Jan van Veldestijn. It was not to be his last address.

Rembrandt wants an address worthy of his reputation

While waiting impatiently for the sum owed to him by the Stadholder, Rembrandt negotiated the purchase of a house built in 1606 in Sint Anthoniesdijk on the Breestraat. It had two principal floors topped by a stepped gable. The owners, Pieter Belten and Christoffel Thijsz, demanded a price of thirteen thousand guilders, not all payable at once. The contract of sale stipulated that Rembrandt must pay a quarter of the amount in three instalments in the first year. The balance was to be paid in five or six years. Any amount outstanding would then incur interest of five per cent. On 1 May 1639 Rembrandt and Saskia moved to their new address. It was next door to the dealer van Ulenborch, in whose house in this new and prosperous district next to the ghetto they had originally met.

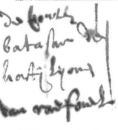

This engraving shows *The House in Sint Anthoniesbreestraat* as Rembrandt would have known it.

It was doubtless because he was raising money for the house that Rembrandt failed to outbid Alphonso Lopez on 9 April. That day Raphael's *Portrait of Baldassare Castiglione* was auctioned at the house of the dealer Lucas van Uffelen.

Rembrandt, reproached for never having been to Italy, discovers Italian art in Amsterdam

During the sale he drew this portrait, noting upon it the selling price of the Raphael, 3500 guilders. The

purchaser, Alphonso Lopez, a Spanish Jew, was a diamond and picture dealer living on the Singelgracht in Amsterdam. He supplied Richelieu and the French court with works of art. In his collection Rembrandt saw a portrait by another Italian master, Titian's *Ariosto*. Lopez also owned a Rembrandt, *Balaam and the Ass*, signed and dated 'RL 1626'. Rembrandt copied Raphael and

R aphael's *Portrait of Baldassare Castiglione,* dated 1516 (above), was copied by Rembrandt in a form of self-portrait (left) in 1639.

Titian, rendering the poses of Baldassare Castiglione and Ariosto in his own manner. It is from paintings that paintings are born.

Rembrandt painted relentlessly in his house in Sint Anthoniesbreestraat. His studio was upstairs, above the family living quarters. Pictures and portfolios of etchings began to accumulate in one of the adjacent rooms, while the other was filled with weapons, exotic garments and curios. On the very top floor were more studios, used by Rembrandt's pupils. There they prepared the mixture of bitumen, beeswax and resin which was used to coat the copper plates; or they made copies of Rembrandt's paintings, which he himself altered and reworked.

As to the fate of those pictures which were neither copies nor originals, no one was much concerned. Authenticity was not an issue. What mattered was to paint.

Cornelia: a name to mourn

A baby, Cornelia, was baptized in July 1638, but she died three weeks later. At the end of 1639 Saskia became pregnant for the third time. Hope rose anew. The daughter, born in July 1640 and again given the name Cornelia, survived only two weeks. Her death was followed by that of Rembrandt's mother, Cornelia, in Leiden. She left an inheritance of 9160 guilders.

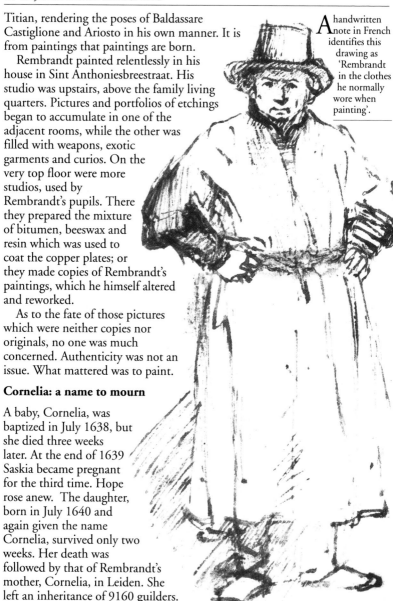

A handwritten note in French identifies this drawing as 'Rembrandt in the clothes he normally wore when painting'.

A few months afterwards Titia, the sister to whom Saskia had probably been closest, died in her turn.

The still-life of a flayed ox painted in Rembrandt's studio early in 1640 is ultimately a religious picture. The dead meat was a comment on human life, far removed in its import from the flesh of the elegant models Rembrandt was painting at the same period. Did anyone understand? They went on looking at his religious paintings.

Despite his grief, Rembrandt continued to work. An Englishman called Peter Mundy who passed through Amsterdam mentioned the name of only one Dutch painter in his travel diary and that was Rembrandt. Johannes Orlers added a note about him in the second edition of his *Description of the Town of Leiden,* published in 1641. Rembrandt's name also attracted a mention in Tommaso Garzoni's *Piazza Universale,* published in Basle by Matthaus Merian.

Like Jacques Callot and Abraham Bosse, he was one of the recognized masters of etching in the 17th century. Rembrandt's fame as a painter and etcher was spreading throughout Europe. The French painter Claude Vignon had seen *Balaam and the Ass,* owned by Alphonso Lopez, and thought highly of it. He sent his respects to Rembrandt and advised a friend of his, who was an art dealer, to bring back some of Rembrandt's work from Amsterdam.

The authenticity of this *Flayed Ox* (1640), striking in its three-dimensional effect, is doubted by some experts. The carcasses of pigs or cattle painted at this period were intended to remind the viewer of the transience of human life and the divine judgment to come.

The power of Rembrandt's portraits

Rembrandt was adulated. But he was not content just to be a fashionable painter. He had portrayed Marten Soolmans and his wife Oepjen Coppit in all their splendour, their gloves, their lace and finery in 1634; he had painted the ruffs of the merchant Willem Burchgraeff and his wife Margaretha Bilderbeeck; he had painted a shipowner, his hand resting on the drawing of a ship, while his wife is delivering him a note. These were 'functional' portraits which were exactly what their patrons wanted.

When in 1640 he painted a pair of portraits of Herman Doomer, framer and gilder, and his wife, Baartjen Martens, he harked back to the portrait of Jan Cornelisz Sylvius, etched in 1633, and that of the preacher Jan Uytenbogaert, etched in 1635. These portraits are not a rendering of

Cornelis Claesz Anslo is the subject of these three portraits by Rembrandt: a drawing (left), a painting (above), an etching (right). A prosperous merchant and a preacher, Anslo belonged to the Mennonite sect which dressed soberly.

Rembrandt often arrived at a painting by careful and unhurried preparatory work. For example in 1640 he drew a portrait of the Mennonite preacher Cornelis Claesz Anslo. In 1641 he developed this into an etching which more precisely rendered the face. The poet Joos van den Vondel wrote: 'Rembrandt really needs to paint Cornelis' voice. His external appearance is what is least representative of him, and what is invisible can only be known by sound: whoever wants to see Anslo should listen to him.' Rembrandt met the challenge. Does the raised hand gesturing to the open book in front of him (opposite) not make his very voice audible? The same year (1641) Rembrandt painted another portrait of Anslo (left), his hand raised in the direction of a woman who is listening to him.

Cornelis Claesz Anslo

the status and role of the sitter, but a musing on his subject. In this portrait of a craftsman Rembrandt was undoubtedly trying to recapture the intensity that marks his then unfinished painting of Cornelis Claesz Anslo. The latter appears at a table piled with books, talking to the woman sitting next to him. Sylvius, Uytenbogaert, Anslo are all shown reading the Bible and preaching.

The first was a Calvinist, the second a member of the Armenian Church, the third a Mennonite. These works of Rembrandt are meditations on the words of the apostles and the prophets.

Light and dark

In order to paint dreams, meditations, thoughts, Rembrandt created a wholly new way of using light. The external world was no longer his subject.

He bought prints all the time and through them studied Italian art. Being black and white, they disclosed nothing of the brilliance of the original canvases and frescos, nor of the materials used. All they revealed was the composition of a work and the arrangement and play of light and shadow.

With his experience of copperplate etching Rembrandt knew the lines to cut with the etcher's needle and the depth of biting necessary to create shadow. His understanding in terms of line and shadow of paintings he had never seen and his practical experience of etching had a decisive influence on his work.

It was not painting but etching that inspired him when he began to organize light and shadow on his canvases. Rembrandt applied chiaroscuro as if he were using ink on paper. By adding colour he gave it a further dimension. This chiaroscuro was not a placing of shadow where light would logically cast it. It was a way of providing emphasis in a picture, of creating the effect the artist desired. If Rembrandt 'lit' a hand and a glove that should properly speaking have been overshadowed by a shoulder, this was because that

The above work, *The Artist Drawing from a Model* (1639), shows a studio crowded with implements, objects and ornaments in the even light.

The light that illuminates the face of Nicolaes Bruyningh (left) and cuts across his cuff and hand is the quintessence of chiaroscuro. The forcefulness of the portrait is Rembrandt's one object, his firm control of light the secret of its power.

hand and glove had a significance in the painting over and above being simple representations.

Over the years Rembrandt abandoned the use of chiaroscuro to achieve dramatic effect. He simultaneously gave up signalling particular details to indicate particular episodes in the Bible. It was enough for him that the arbitrary use of chiaroscuro should serve only the ends of the painting itself.

Rembrandt and Saskia's happiness is increased by a new commission

On 22 September 1641, at the Zuiderkerk, the fourth child of Saskia and Rembrandt was baptized. He was given the name Titus. Anxious weeks went by, but Titus did not die.

Frans Banning Cocq, meanwhile, was ambitious. His marriage had provided him with the requisite means. He inhabited one of the finest buildings on the

The figure with his hand on his hip, is Frans Banning Cocq (1605–55), a prominent personality in Amsterdam society. Thanks to his marriage to the burgomaster's daughter, he became very rich and acquired, in addition to a number of properties, the title of Lord of Purmerland. He was later ennobled by James II. This portrait of him is a detail taken from *The Governors of the Honourable Archers' Guild in Amsterdam* by Bartholomeus van der Helst. Realized over ten years after Rembrandt's *Night Watch*, it was no doubt exactly what Cocq wanted, presenting him elegantly posed, surrounded by works of art.

Singelgracht, designed by the architect Hendrick de Keyser. He had soon become part of the city hierarchy, and served a term as burgomaster. His military career as an officer had been no less successful. After peace was established, when war was no longer waged on Dutch soil but only at sea, the militia, the civil guard and their companies had little to do but parade and take part in shooting competitions.

A political career like Cocq's was not to pass unsung. The militia officers had defended the towns and founded the republic. They had won lasting prestige. At the end of 1640 Frans Banning Cocq and the officers of his company had commissioned Rembrandt to paint their group portrait, completed in 1642.

In the meantime Saskia was making a poor recovery from the birth.

The portrait of the company is to hang in a room in the new wing of the Kloveniersdoelen

Group portraits of the militia belonged to a tradition longer even than that of anatomy lessons. Once again Rembrandt's painting had to surpass the works of his predecessors – and also outshine the portraits commissioned by five other companies: from Joachim von Sandrart, by the company of Captain Cornelis Bicker; from Govaert Flinck (a former pupil), by the company of Captain Bas; from Bartholomeus van der Helst, by the company of Captain Roelof Bicker; from Nicolaes Eliasz Pickenoy, by that of Captain van Vlooswijck, and lastly from Jacob Adriaensz Backer (another of his pupils), by that of Captain De Graeff.

Saskia was utterly exhausted.

Rembrandt had painted, drawn and etched Saskia in many guises, smiling, compliant, patient, triumphant. Then in 1641 he etched *Saskia Ill, with Large White Headdress* (above left), portraying her in a state of utter exhaustion, her rounded cheeks sunken, her eyes fixed on empty space. Was it premonition that in 1639 had led Rembrandt to etch *Youth Surprised by Death* and *The Death of the Virgin*, realized after sketches of *Saskia Lying Ill in Bed* (detail above)?

AMSTERDA
met d'uytlegging van 't Iaer

Den Amstel

HET

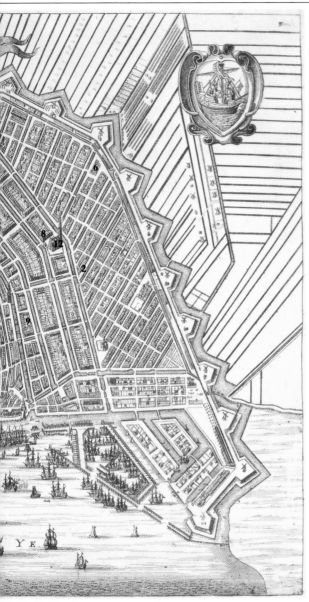

Map of Rembrandt's Amsterdam:

1. House of the painter Pieter Lastman, under whom Rembrandt studied in 1624.

2. House in the Doelstraat, where he lived with Saskia until 1636.

3. The Bloemgracht, where Rembrandt set up studio in 1635.

4. District of Binnen Amstel, where Rembrandt lived until 1639.

5. House in Sint Anthoniesdijk on the Breestraat. Bought by Rembrandt and Saskia in 1639, sold at auction in 1658.

6. House in the Rozengracht, where Rembrandt spent the last ten years of his life.

7. House inhabited by Titus on the Singelgracht after his marriage to Magdalena van Loo.

8. House of Professor Tulp on the Keizersgracht.

9. House of Captain Cocq on the Singelgracht.

10. Probably Jan Six's residence on the Kloveniersburgwal.

11. Keizerskroon Inn, where all Rembrandt's possessions were sold at auction.

12. Westerkerk, the church where Rembrandt and his family were buried.

Rembrandt was to receive 1600 guilders for this painting. Each of the sixteen guards paid more or less than 100 guilders, depending on the place he occupied in the composition. It was not a very large sum for a group portrait. Indeed much more had been paid in Holland for a tulip bulb. It is possible of course that the officers paid a supplement not mentioned in the contract.

Saskia stayed in bed, ill.

Rembrandt devotes himself entirely to the painting, for weeks, then months

Very early in the year 1642 the portrait was delivered to Kloveniersdoelen. The title of the work, as inscribed in a sketchbook containing a watercolour reproduction, was *The young Heer van Purmerandt [Banning Cocq] as Captain, Ordering his Lieutenant, the Heer van Vlaerdingen [Willem van Ruytenburch], to March the Company out.*

Twelve years after Rembrandt's death Filippo Baldinucci wrote: 'He won greater renown than any practitioner of this art. The reason was that among the figures shown a captain had one foot lifted as if in midstep, and held in his hand a halberd in such well-drawn perspective that, while it hardly exceeded half a *braccio* [*c.* 30 centimetres] on the canvas, it looked to everybody as if it were lifesize; the other figures, it is true, were mixed and mingled in such a fashion that it was difficult readily to distinguish one from another, however carefully they might have been painted from life.'

On 5 June 1642 Saskia draws up her last will and testament

Saskia left approximately forty thousand guilders to Rembrandt and Titus. Half was to revert to Titus. Rembrandt had a life interest until his son came of age or married. But this clause became null and void if Rembrandt remarried. Saskia did not require Rembrandt

In 1715 Rembrandt's painting *The Company of Captain Frans Banning Cocq* (right) was cut down on all sides so that it could hang on the second floor of the Nieuwe Stadhuis, later to become the Royal Palace. Roughly 25 cm was removed on the top and 15 cm on the bottom, 30 cm on the left and 10 cm on the right: the painting had to fit between the two doors.

s dust and the ravages of age darkened its tones, Rembrandt's painting of Captain Cocq's Company (left) came to be known as *The Night Watch.*

to draw up an inventory of his assets and, in a final clause, she appointed Rembrandt sole guardian to Titus and refused to let Titus' affairs be run by the Court of Orphans.

On 14 June Saskia died, probably from tuberculosis. She was thirty years old. Five days later she was buried. On 9 July her remains were taken to the Oudekerk, where Rembrandt had bought a tomb. Titus was barely a year old. Neither Saskia's sister nor Rembrandt's mother were alive to look after him. Commissions were pouring in from all directions.

In 1642 *The Company of Captain Frans Banning Cocq* brought Rembrandt growing renown, while his private life fell to pieces with Saskia's death.

Is *The Sick Man of Samaria* (below), attended by doctors, not in fact a dying woman (opposite: *Saskia Lying Ill in Bed*)? Rembrandt exorcized his grief and anxiety by giving them artistic expression.

" This painting, whatever the criticisms of it may be, will survive all its competitors because it is so painterly in conception, so ingenious in its varied arrangement of figures, and so powerful that in comparison, according to some, all other paintings there look like playing cards." This was the opinion of Samuel van Hoogstraten on *The Company of Captain Frans Banning Cocq*, also known as *The Night Watch*.

CHAPTER 3

LONELINESS AND BANKRUPTCY

In *The Night Watch* (detail opposite) the eyes gazing beyond the blade of a sword, removed, slightly knowing, are Rembrandt's. A very different tone is set by *The Slippers* (right), painted by Rembrandt's pupil Samuel van Hoogstraten.

Nobody doubted Rembrandt's genius. Indeed it was because nobody doubted it that people made criticisms. The terms in which they did so, however, given that he depended entirely on commissions, proved highly damaging. He was accused of painting 'too much to please himself': an artist was expected to meet the requirements of those who commissioned his work. Rembrandt might have produced a work of art, but what he had been engaged to do was paint a group portrait, no more, no less. This amounted to false pretences.

The genius that dazzles art lovers and collectors does not stop clients from quibbling

It was not genius that clients paid for but an identifiable image: a portrait should be a 'likeness'. Rembrandt, on the other hand, was painting an inner self, an elusive essence, a metamorphosis. Flinck, Bol, Backer, and other pupils of his besides, began to find more acceptance with the public than their master. Rembrandt's driving desire was simply to paint, to test the limits of his art.

A few months after Saskia's death he painted a portrait of her as a pair to a self-portrait signed and dated 'Rembrandt f 1643'. In this picture he is defying death: painted, he and Saskia stand together, eternalized as art. A portrait like this was akin to painting the mysteries of the Old and New Testament: the same subjects, death and resurrection, were given expression by his brush. In Rembrandt's mind *seeing* was indeed *believing*.

Geertge Dircx, Titus' nurse, drawn by Rembrandt *c.* 1642.

Genius wins him respect and admiration. But acceptance?

Whether or not he was accepted did not concern Rembrandt. He painted. As for the rest....

Rembrandt engaged a nurse to look after Titus. She was a stalwart countrywoman from the north called Geertge Dircx, the widow of Abraham Claeszoon, a trumpeter.

This left Rembrandt free to concentrate on etching. He found subjects everywhere: the slanting rays across

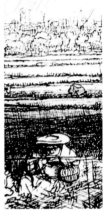

The storm passes over the summer sky of *The Three Trees* (left, with detail above), etched by Rembrandt in 1643. The opposition of light and shade, startling in its precision, conveys both stillness and energy.

a lightly clouded sky in this landscape, *The Three Trees*, a pig lying down, a scholar lost in thought, a monk knocking over a girl in the corn, subjects from the Old and New Testaments, beggars and naked men. He did not tailor his inspiration to the norms of Calvinist good taste. His models dreamed, prayed or sinned. As he himself painted, prayed and sinned. He took his young son's nurse as his mistress.

It was not Rembrandt who named this etching *Le Lit à la française*. He does not seem to be interested in social observation.

The words attributed to Rembrandt by Houbraken have the ring of truth: 'When I wish to occupy my mind, I do not care so much for honour as I do for liberty.' But Rembrandt had more to do than pass judgment on his own life. He lived for and through his painting. Everything was subordinate to his art, and dedicated to it.

By the end of the 1640s Rembrandt is painting fewer commissioned portraits

Old men daydreaming, bedecked in chains, caps upon their heads, young girls in reverie, elbows propped at a window, or hands upon a door, were subjects that did not need to be 'commissioned'. Nor did paintings of stories from the Bible. Thus Rembrandt painted *The Woman Taken in Adultery, The Holy Family with the Curtain, The Adoration of the Shepherds, Joseph's Dream* and *Anna Accused by Tobit of Stealing the Kid. The Woman Taken in Adultery* was bought by the Stadholder, also a *Circumcision.* He paid 2400 guilders for these two works in November 1646. In shape and size they were very like those he had bought seven years earlier. Whereas he had previously commissioned paintings, he was now buying finished works. This signified a change in Rembrandt's relationship with his clients.

Anecdotes that were recorded long after Rembrandt's death and so should be treated as unconfirmed...

The first is recounted by Baldinucci: 'After it had become commonly known that whoever wanted to be portrayed by him had to sit to him for some two or three months, there were few who came forward. The cause of his slowness was that, immediately after the first work had dried, he took it up again, repainting it with bigger or smaller strokes.... When he worked he would not have granted an audience to the first monarch in the world, who would have had to return and return again until he had found him no longer engaged upon that work.'

The second is related by Houbraken: 'He often drew

Is St Jerome beside a Pollard Willow (below) engaged in translating the Bible? Rembrandt etched this appealing image of the hermit's life in 1648.

In these two paintings, both subjects drawn from the Christian faith, Rembrandt used theatrical elements rarely found in his work. In *Christ at Emmaus* (above) a stone alcove frames the figure of Christ, while the open curtain in *The Holy Family with the Curtain* (left) serves to frame the scene like a stage set, a device used in antique painting.

ten versions of a face before reproducing one on the canvas, where he could spend an entire day, even two, determining the arrangement of a turban in the way that most pleased him.'

The last anecdote also comes from Houbraken: 'One day he was working on a large group portrait featuring a couple and their children. He had nearly finished it when his monkey died: not having another canvas to hand, he included the dead monkey in the work in progress. Naturally his models could scarcely tolerate the unappetizing relic featured at their side; but the effect produced by the corpse so impressed the artist that rather than remove it to satisfy his clients he left the work unfinished.'

Rembrandt's demands become intolerable to the 'clients' he is supposed to 'satisfy': they abandon him

Rembrandt made do without his clients, as they forsook him. His life began to be characterized by extravagance, even scandal. He was constantly buying – in salerooms, from dealers, pedlars, sellers of old clothes.

'He began to buy old clothes that struck him as strange and picturesque; and even when they were utterly filthy he hung them on the wall in his workshop, amidst the beautiful curiosities he had taken pleasure in collecting, such as ancient and modern weapons of all kinds: arrows, halberds, daggers, swords, knives, an inordinate quantity of prints, medals and exquisite drawings, and many other objects he thought might be of use to a painter. At the same time he deserves much praise for a particular generosity, however extravagant it might have been in reality. He held his art in such high esteem that when anything connected with it was offered at auction, such as paintings and drawings by great artists in various fields, he put in such a high offer that nobody could outbid him; and he said that he did this to build up the prestige of his profession.'

There seems no reason to doubt the hearsay reports recounted by Baldinucci. Saskia had left an inheritance

This portrait is thought to be of Rembrandt's son Titus, born in 1641, which would suggest a date of 1650 for the picture.

of 40,750 guilders. That Rembrandt should have spent a part of it buying old materials and objects supposedly needed for his painting – or for the prestige of his profession – was regarded, at best, as irresponsible. The Amsterdam of money markets, banks and businesses did not approve of extravagance.

Irresponsible and debauched

Calvinist Amsterdam looked askance at any hint of debauchery. The young Hendrickje Stoffelsdochter Jaegher (usually known as Hendrickje Stoffels) had been living in the house in Sint Anthoniesdijk for some time before she became Rembrandt's mistress in 1649. This development was not welcomed by Geertge Dircx, who had previously filled the role. On 24 January 1648 she had dictated a will appointing Titus her heir. All her assets, including Saskia's jewelry, which Rembrandt had given her, were left to him.

This drawing (c. 1642) of a woman in the peasant dress of northern Holland is thought to be a *Portrait of Geertge Dircx*, Titus' nurse and Rembrandt's mistress. She caused many problems for the artist and he seems not to have painted her very often.

This will was put forward as evidence a few months later when she brought a case of breach of promise against Rembrandt. The tribunal dismissed her action, but set a figure of 200 guilders per year to be paid by Rembrandt to Geertge Dircx in compensation for rescinding the revocation of her will. (Rembrandt had offered 166 guilders.)

Some time afterwards he tried to recover Saskia's jewelry. Crippled with debt, Geertge had pawned all the pieces. Rembrandt took her before the court and accused her of a dissolute life. On 23 October 1649 she was condemned to twelve years of solitary confinement with hard labour. Rembrandt was made responsible for the cost of transporting her to Gouda, where she was

to be locked away, and he had to continue paying her allowance.

Rembrandt besieged by jealous spirits

Hendrickje Stoffels had been a witness in the case. She was twenty-four years old, possibly only twenty-three. Rembrandt was twenty years older. He made no attempt to hide the fact that she lived with him as his wife. Like everyone in his entourage, she even posed for him. But he did not marry her, as this would have meant renouncing his life interest in the inheritance left to him by Saskia. Rembrandt went on spending. He began to fall into debt. The former owners of the house in Sint Anthoniesdijk had still not been paid in full.

His reputation as an artist remained untarnished by court proceedings and his financial situation. Lambert van den Bos wrote a poem in 1650 acclaiming the collection of Marten Kretzer, which included works by Titian and Rubens: 'I shall not drive myself to prove your renown, O Rembrandt, with the scratches of my

The Sleeping Nymph and a Satyr in the drawing above are a veiled allusion to Titian's *Jupiter and Antiope.*

There is the hint of a smile on the face of this elegant woman. A muted brilliance lights only her face, the pearls of her jewelry and her bosom. The look in her eyes betrays intimacy with the artist. The portrait is generally thought to be of Hendrickje Stoffels. She posed for Rembrandt in the same way as Saskia, whose place and role she had assumed.

pen, as the esteem in which you are held everywhere emerges with the sole mention of your name.'

Nonetheless there was no escaping the two experts who came during the year 1650 to make an inventory of Rembrandt's chattels in Sint Anthoniesdijk. His collections were valued at 17,000 guilders. Of the total, Rembrandt's own paintings accounted for 6400 guilders. His capital value perhaps reassured his creditors. For the moment they took no further action.

Merchants and politicians forsake his studio. Men of a more intellectual bent are drawn there instead

With the passage of years those most often to be found in Rembrandt's company seemed to be given to writing, study, commentary, painting, creativity. Jan Cornelisz Sylvius was a theologian and preacher. Hendrick Martensz Sorgh was a painter. Dr Ephraim Bueno was one of the foremost Jewish doctors and writers

Rembrandt concentrated on etching landscapes in the year 1650, with the exception of *The Shell* (above). The image perhaps symbolized the riches brought by foreign trade; however, it seems more likely that Rembrandt was fascinated by the perfect structure of its spirals, the patterned smoothness of its surface.

in Amsterdam. Rembrandt etched or painted their portraits.

Jan Six aspired to more than the status of burgomaster of Amsterdam. He wrote poetry and tragedies. In 1648, the year after Rembrandt etched the first portrait of him, standing with his back to the window reading, he published a long tragedy in verse, *Medea*. He

belonged to a noble family that had fled St Omer in northern France, which had expelled the Huguenots. He had studied at the university of Leiden and done a Grand Tour of Italy in 1640. In 1652 he gave up business. Sometimes he invited Rembrandt to stay in an estate he owned on the Diemerdyke. There Rembrandt drew landscapes and did two drawings in Six's *Album amicorum*.

The man writing at an open window, his face concealed by the brim of his hat, is *Jan Six at his Desk*, a drawing by Rembrandt dated 1655. In 1652 Jan Six had retired from business to devote himself to writing. He is also featured, leaning over the bridge reading, in Rembrandt's etching *Six's Bridge* (below left), dated 1645.

Like Rembrandt, Jan Six collected antiques, enamels and other objets d'art. But the means at their disposal were different.

1652. Rembrandt's creditors grow uneasy

Might they have been placated by the news that a nobleman from Messina, Don Antonio Ruffo, had commissioned a work from him: 'a philosopher', without further specification? It seems unlikely. Rembrandt talking painting. They talked money. That he painted was of no interest to them: what he had to do was pay.

By 1653 some of his creditors could wait no longer. The United Netherlands had suffered setbacks in the war against England and crisis ensued. The stock exchange was in trouble. Rembrandt had to borrow money. Jan Six lent 1000 guilders. Lodewijk van Ludick stood guarantor. Cornelis Witsen, former burgomaster of Amsterdam, and the merchant Isaac van Heertsbeeck each lent 4000 guilders. All Rembrandt's assets were offered as security for these loans, possibly including his paintings. The *Portrait of Saskia in a Red Hat* and *St John the Baptist Preaching* joined Jan Six's collection. Rembrandt never managed to finish paying for his house in Sint Anthoniesdijk. In February 1653, through a notary, Christoffel Thijsz had presented an account of 8470 guilders, interest included, being the outstanding debt.

The auditors grow rich at the expense of the creditors

Hendrickje and Rembrandt were summoned to appear before the ecclesiastical court. There they were to answer accusations of living together unmarried.

They refused. In July 1654 the consistory of the Calvinist Church cited Hendrickje again, and she alone. Why was Rembrandt not accused? We have no answer. His name did not figure either in the registers of the Mennonite Church, which he was supposed to have joined. Hendrickje received many more summonses, which she ignored. When at last she appeared before the judges, she was exhorted to renounce her illicit relationship and do penance. She continued to live with Rembrandt. In October 1654, in the Oudekerk where Saskia had been laid to rest, a daughter of Rembrandt and Hendrickje was baptized, and named Cornelia.

Both in its size (38.5 x 45 cm) and in its dramatic use of the effects of light and shade, *The Three Crosses* (1653) ranks as one of Rembrandt's most important etchings. Above are the first version (left) and a detail from the fourth version (right). Opposite: *The Woman Taken in Adultery*.

In 1654 Rembrandt again fails to meet his debts

Once again he had to negotiate an agreement with Thijsz. He pledged a yearly payment of 50 guilders. Thijsz could hardly have been under any illusion. He knew that Rembrandt had few commissions and the sums he was paid for them. Cornelis Eysbert van Goor, who had acted as intermediary between the painter and the Sicilian noble, had sent Rembrandt 500 guilders for *Aristotle Contemplating the Bust of Homer*, the 'philosopher' commissioned in 1652. The canvas

L acking the legal status of wife to Rembrandt, Hendrickje's name is never officially linked to his pictures. Her face and figure nonetheless featured in a good many of them, which were euphemistically given titles such as *Woman Looking out of the Window* (above).

is signed and dated 1653. Months of work had been involved. As for other work, Thijsz must have been aware that Rembrandt refused to comply with some of his clients' requirements.

For example, Diego Andrada, a Sephardi merchant, commissioned a portrait of a girl, for which he paid 65 guilders on account. The rest was to be paid on delivery of the painting. Andrada did not find that there was any likeness and asked to be reimbursed. Intolerant of criticism, Rembrandt replied by demanding the rest of his fee. Clients were not willing to accept his intransigence.

F or centuries *The Polish Rider* (above left) was accepted as the work of Rembrandt. In recent years, however, doubts have been cast by some experts on its authenticity. Another 'Rembrandt' to be removed from the catalogue of the artist's works is *The Man with the Golden Helmet.*

By May 1656 Rembrandt is in desperate straits

On 17 May he applied to the Court of Orphans
to transfer the title deeds of the house in Sint
Anthoniesdijk to Titus. He agreed to remain responsible
for all debts. The court refused. One of Rembrandt's
brothers was declared a pauper in Leiden and his
sister was close to insolvency.

The court appointed a guardian to determine the
respective shares of Titus and his father.

On 20 July 1656 the High Court appointed Frans
Janszoon Bruningh to liquidate Rembrandt's assets.

Rembrandt painted
Bathsheba in 1654.
Bathsheba, suffering
David's cruelty, and
Hendrickje, hounded by
the Church, were linked
by a spirit of forced
resignation.

Overleaf left: *A
Woman Bathing in
a Stream.* Overleaf right:
*Hendrickje at the
Window.*

The painter had successfully petitioned the court to apply the principle of a *cessio bonorum*. This was generally done only for debtors of acknowledged good faith. The pretext of damages and losses suffered at sea was accepted by the court, sparing Rembrandt the disgrace of a fraudulent bankruptcy and prison sentence.

On 25 and 26 July 1656 an inventory of the entire contents of the house in Sint Anthoniesbreestraat is prepared

The list comprised 363 items (see pp. 130–5). Everything was scrupulously written down. The 'linen at the laundry', nos. 359-63; 'a pewter water jug', no. 351; 'a sculpture of the Emperor Augustus', no. 147; '2 pillows', no. 133; 'an East Indian sewing box', no. 150; '47 specimens of land and sea animals and the like', no. 175; 'a portrait head by Raphael of Urbino',

Dangling a pencil case in front of his desk, Titus, seems to be lost in thought, perhaps about his next drawing. The inventory of Rembrandt's possessions mentioned 'three little dogs done from life by Titus van Rijn'. Also listed was a book of drawings by Titian, including two studies for *The Death of St Peter Martyr* reproduced opposite. Below is a drawing by Rembrandt of the parable of *The Unjust Steward.*

no. 67; 'a book filled with drawings of all Roman buildings and views by all the most excellent masters', no. 240; 'a small [model of?] a metal cannon', no. 335; 'A "Raising of Lazarus" by Jan Lievensz', no. 42....

A fabulous collection of paintings by Adriaen Brouwer, Jan Lievens, Hercules Seghers, Palma Vecchio, Pieter Lastman, Govaert Jansz Flinck, Jan Porcellis, Lucas van Valckenburgh, Jacopo Bassano, Raphael, Jan van Eyck, Giorgione.... A fabulous collection of tens of portfolios full of engravings by Pieter Bruegel the Elder, Lucas Cranach the Elder, Antonio Tempesta, Lucas van Leyden, Rubens, Jacob Jordaens, Jacques Callot.... A fabulous collection of engraved reproductions of works by Titian, Raphael, Michelangelo, Annibale Carracci, Giovanni Battista Rosso ('Fiorentino') and Giulio Bonasone.... The house in which Rembrandt painted was packed with masterpieces.

On the point of being stripped of all his possessions, Rembrandt paints a second anatomy lesson

Professor Tholinx was a relation of Jan Six and of Professor Tulp. It was doubtless at his suggestion that Dr Johannes Deyman, who succeeded him as Inspector of the Medical Colleges in Amsterdam, commissioned another anatomy lesson from Rembrandt. The lessons were now held in the lecture-room to which *The Anatomy Lesson of Professor Tulp* had been removed. Deyman's portrait was to hang in the same room. The first anatomy lesson had brought Rembrandt fame and fortune in Amsterdam. Twenty-four years later he had to prove that, in spite of adversity, he remained the greatest painter in Holland.

Deyman based his lesson on the mortal remains of a certain Joris Fonteyn de Diest. Originally, on either side of the prone corpse, there were eight men. At the doctor's side his assistant Gysbrecht Matthysz Calckoen held the top of the skull. Sir Joshua Reynolds, who saw the canvas before a fire in Sint Anthonieswaag in 1723 destroyed three-quarters of it, observed that the colours resembled those of Titian.

Titian is not the only artist of the Italian Renaissance evoked by the painting. The way the corpse is laid out recalls Mantegna's *Dead Christ*. The inventory of Rembrandt's chattels mentioned, at item no. 200, 'the precious book of Andrea Mantegna'.

The auction of Rembrandt's possessions starts in September 1656

The curiosities were sold. The paintings went under the hammer in December 1657. Disputes between the creditors then stopped further sales for some months. In February 1658 the house in Sint Anthoniesdijk went for 11,218 guilders. This sum, by no means negligible in a recession, did not, however, cover Rembrandt's debts.

In September 1658 the collection of prints and drawings was sold, despite attempts to preserve it. The sale was advertised: 'The administrator of the property of the painter Rembrandt van Rijn has been authorized by their Honours, the Commissioners of the Chamber

E Curateur ober den Infol=
venten Boedel van Rembrant van Rijn / konstigh
Schilder / sal / als by de E. E herren Commissari=
sen der Desolate Boedelen hier ter Stede daer toe ge=
authoriseert / by Executie verkopen de voorsz Papier
Kunst onder den selven Boedel als noch berustende/
bestaende inde Konst van ber ccheydem der voomaruiste so Italiaenscher/
Franscher/ Duytscher ende Nederlandscher Meesters / ende by den selven
Rembrant van Rijn met een groote curieusheyt te samen versamelt.

Gelijck dan mede een goede partye van
Teeckeningen ende Schetsen vanden selven Rembrant van Rijn selven

De verkopinge sal wesen ten daeghe/
ure ende Jaere als boven / ten huyse van
Barent Jansz Schuurman / Waert in
de Keysers Kroon / inde Kalver straet/
daer de verkopinge voor desen is geweest.

Segget voort.

This notice advertised the sale of Rembrandt's collection of prints and drawings at the Keizerskroon Inn in September 1658.

A fire in 1723 destroyed three-quarters of *The Anatomy Lesson of Dr Johannes Deyman* (opposite). Of Deyman, only the hands remain visible and of the eight spectators originally positioned in symmetrical fashion round the surgeon, only his assistant survives, holding the top of the corpse's skull in his left hand. More accurately informed than in 1632, Rembrandt this time featured the dissected abdomen.

of Insolvent Estates, to sell by executive order the works of art, in said estate, consisting of works by various prominent Italian, French, German, and Netherlandish masters which the said Rembrandt van Rijn has assembled by his care. At the same time, a large number of drawings and sketches by the said Rembrandt van Rijn himself will be offered for sale. The sale will take place on the day, hour and year stated above, at the house of Barent Jansz Schuurman, innkeeper of the Keizerskroon [The Emperor's Crown], on the Calverstraat, where the previous sale was held.'

The sale took place. Everything was dispersed. For the derisory sum of 600 guilders.

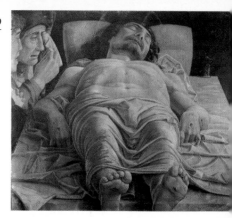

Rembrandt owned an engraving of Mantegna's *Dead Christ* (above), which was the model for *The Anatomy Lesson of Dr Johannes Deyman* (below).

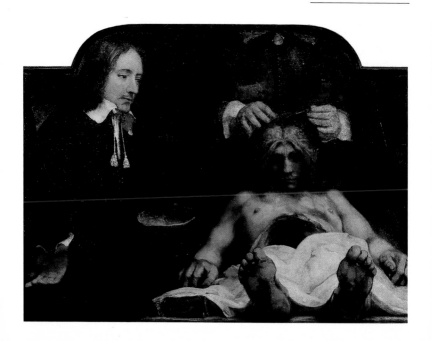

In the denuded house in Sint Anthoniesdijk that no longer belonged to him Rembrandt read the eulogies that the poet Jeremias de Decker had heaped on his work in *De Hollandsche Parnas*, published in 1660, and the verses by H. F. Waterloos extolling his portrait of Jeremias de Decker. Did his bankruptcy, reputation and alienation worry him? Ruined, idolized, rejected, he still knew his own worth.

CHAPTER 4
RETIREMENT AND DEATH

The *Self-portrait* (detail opposite) of Rembrandt in a heavy coat with a wide brown collar, a white cap upon the tangle of his grizzled locks, was painted *c.* 1663. The circles in the background represent time. The portrait of the artist's son, *Titus Reading* (left), was done a few years earlier.

The very year (1658) that he was stripped in the auction rooms of all that had once represented his ambition, he painted a self-portrait: seated, grave, serene, he holds a cane in the fingers of his left hand. It is a portrait of self-assurance and power, a portrait of Rembrandt's pride. At the end of the day it mattered little to him that nothing was left. He could still paint.

Rembrandt in the mirror of art

It was not the first self-portrait or the last. He painted, drew or etched his own portrait approximately one hundred times. No other artist has matched him in this. He featured himself in 1625 in the crowd stoning St Stephen, in 1626 with a harp in his hands (in *A Musical Gathering*), in 1665 bursting with laughter as Zeuxis, the painter of antiquity. He showed himself in all moods: apprehensive, mirthful, debonair, confident, conceited, arrogant, disillusioned. He painted the onset of the years, puffy features, wrinkles, the ravages of age. It mattered little to him: his portraits did not aim for likeness. In rags or in finery, it was isolation that he studied; an isolation which he tried, perhaps despairingly, to counter with an assurance that proved elusive.

Rembrandt's self-portraits were not a narrative of his life, but the incarnation of his ambitions as a painter. His portraits were studies in which he used his own face to explore a range of expressions, of attitudes, as if drawing up a catalogue. His portraits are declarations. Creating his own version of a Titian or Raphael, he

No model was ever more readily or more freely available to Rembrandt than his own face. He executed an abundance of self-portraits. This was not only a way of studying the range of expression on a face and exploring different artistic techniques. It was also a form of quest and affirmation, a plea, a cry, a record of a lifetime's changing attitudes and emotions. It is impossible to be precise about the number of Rembrandt's self-portraits. Perhaps he did a hundred or so.... Some may well have been copies by his pupils, or copies which he himself revised, or contemporary 'fakes', or different versions of the same portrait done by his own hand. All of which makes a definitive catalogue an impossibility.

F rom left to right: *Self-portrait, Leaning Forward, as if Listening* (1628); *Self-portrait with a Broad Nose* (1628); *Self-portrait in Fur Cap and Light Dress* (1630); *Self-portrait Angry* (1630); *Self-portrait Open-mouthed, as if Shouting* (1630); *Self-portrait in a Soft Cap* (1634).

A self-portrait (1658) shows Rembrandt seated in solitary splendour, confident, with furrowed brow, a smile hesitating at the corners of his lips (left). His left hand holds a cane or a sceptre. How should one interpret these enigmatic trappings? Ruined, Rembrandt was nonetheless declaring his indestructible strength.

proved he knew the great masters, the landmarks in the history of art. His portraits are prayers. He painted himself as a sinner helping to raise the cross upon which Christ was laid, and as a prodigal son.

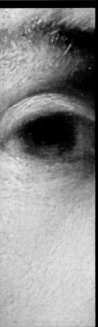

Rembrandt upright, confident, unconquered

In these two self-portraits – dated 1629 (far left and detail above) and 1634 (left) – Rembrandt is wearing the same piece of armour: a steel neck-piece which he used to identifiy himself with the soldier citizens of the United Provinces, who had just won freedom for their country. He had not served as an officer in any militia, but it was a form of patriotism that he shared with many of his clients.

The master

Wearing the familiar broad cap, decked with gold, furs, velvet, embroideries, Rembrandt rests his arm on a narrow parapet in this *Self-portrait* of 1640. His pose is that of Baldassare Castiglione in the portrait by Raphael, which he had copied at the auction where the dealer Alphonso Lopez acquired the work. In the suavity of his Venetian colours he also evokes another picture in Lopez's possession: the painting by Titian of a man in blue sleeves, often entitled *Portrait of Ariosto*. Rembrandt thus appropriated and assimilated the 'inventions' of the Italian artists for this portrait painted in Amsterdam. A sojourn in Italy was not indispensable...

The last years

In these three self-portraits from the 1660s, there are no extraneous trappings, no pomp. The hair has gone grey. The skin has become wrinkled and plump. A look in the eye speaks of weariness and regret, but remains impassive. Rembrandt added gold lines to the white cap, bringing it into harmony with the background, the hair, the skin of the face, as if the painter was merging into his painting.

He painted to save his soul and his reputation. His portraits are portraits of a quest, of his isolation. He was powerless and alone, except for his art.

Money is a continual problem for Rembrandt

In 1658 Rembrandt still owed the 1000 guilders lent to him by Jan Six in 1653. The debt had passed into the hands of a merchant and collector, Lodewijk van Ludick, who required the money, interest and capital, to be repaid in three years plus a painting as a form of supplementary dividend. Rembrandt did not meet either of these conditions.

Rembrandt was no longer concerned with the legal issues outstanding but with Titus' entitlement. Some of the creditors, considering themselves hard done by, were claiming that the 1647 valuation had overestimated Titus' share of the inheritance.

Witnesses were called to prove it valid. The judges took evidence from two men who had paid 100 guilders for their portraits in *The Company of Captain Frans Banning Cocq*, from van Ludick who had bought a Rubens from Rembrandt, from the artist Philips Koninck, and from the silversmith Jan van Loo and his wife who gave a description of Saskia's jewelry. The judges were favourably convinced by the evidence.

On 18 December 1660 Rembrandt leaves the house in Sint Anthoniesbreestraat: all is sold, judgment rendered, debts settled

He spent several days in the Keizerskroon Inn, the very place where his collections of drawings and etchings had been sold in 1657 and 1658. Then he moved into a narrow house on the Rozengracht in the Jordaan district, inhabited by artisans and shopkeepers. It lay in the west

Jan Six (above), whom Rembrandt etched in 1647, had often saved him from bankruptcy. But now he had made over his notes of credit to others. Rembrandt's worldly goods were sold in the Keizerskroon Inn (below).

Rembrandt took his son as the model for this portrait, *Titus in Friar's Habit* of 1660. Did he portray Titus in this way for the pleasure of exploring every shade of brown on the sackcloth robe? Or did he wish to direct the gaze of the viewer to the paleness of the face? Or did he simply think Titus a suitable model for St Francis of Assisi?

of the town beyond the Keizersgracht, the outer of the three canals around the centre of the city.

In this house, rented for 225 guilders a year, he returned to his painting. On 15 December, three days before leaving the Breestraat, he had countersigned an agreement, drawn up by a notary, which made Titus and Hendrickje responsible for him. The rules of the Guild of St Luke, the association of painters which Rembrandt had joined in 1634, left him no alternative: his bankruptcy debarred him from trading in the city. Titus and Hendrickje undertook to feed, lodge and help Rembrandt, who in turn had to acknowledge them as his creditors. He owed 800 guilders to one, 950 guilders to the other. All his work – canvases, drawings, etchings – was to be theirs until his death. And it was to remain at their disposal for a further six years afterwards.

The occasional pupil came to Rembrandt, one being Aert de Gelder, and the occasional portrait was commissioned. He was unconcerned, painting Jacob Jacobsz Trip as he would have painted an apostle.

The faces he painted at this period, whether of Christ, saints, rabbis, men or women, evoke solitude and a calm gravity, a state of mind akin to Rembrandt's own. His work was giving expression to legends and visions, haunted by images from the Bible.

The city of Amsterdam commissions him to paint a vision of a different kind: the national pride of Holland

The commission had first been given to Govaert Flinck, Rembrandt's former pupil, who died having done only a rough sketch. The painting, *The Conspiracy of Julius Civilis*, was supposed to demonstrate the strength of Holland's will to independence, proved in the revolt against Rome and then Spain. The Dutch identified their recent struggles with the revolt of the Batavians against the Romans as recounted by Tacitus. It was at a banquet given by their leader Julius Civilis that the Batavians had sworn to put an end to Roman occupation.

The finished work was to hang in the Burgerzaal of the town hall, opened in 1655.

In 1662 Rembrandt's painting is placed in position, only to be taken down a few months later

The Conspiracy of Julius Civilis was returned to Rembrandt. Another painting was then commissioned from Joris Ovens who reverted to Flinck's sketch, representing Civilis in profile.

What did the elect of Amsterdam dislike in Rembrandt's work? Was it the way the light falling on the array of arms held out over the table exposed Civilis' defunct eye? Legends should not feature the one-eyed. A symbol should be without blemish. Pride knew no handicap. Perhaps there were objections to the way the paint was applied: the rough marks of the palette-knife did not accord with the note of ostentation that was desired.

Rediscovered in 1891 in a Stockholm museum under another title, *The Conspiracy of Julius Civilis* (above and detail far left) represents only a quarter of the original composition. Was this the result of fire, or a deliberate attempt to diminish the power and realism of the scene? An impression of the scale of the original work is given in Rembrandt's preparatory drawing (left).

Rembrandt was left to cut down the canvas of some six metres square and reduce it to more saleable proportions.

Rembrandt's manner of painting upsets his clients and even troubles art lovers

Some years after his death, in *Discourse on the Lives and Works of the Most Excellent Ancient and Modern Painters*, published in 1685, the French writer André Félibien wrote: 'All his works are painted in a very individual manner, very different from that ordinarily used by Flemish painters, which seems so overrefined. For he often uses large brushstrokes, and applies thick layers of colour, one after the other, without blending and softening them. Nevertheless, as tastes vary, a number of people have formed a high opinion of his work.'

Early in the 18th century Arnold Houbraken observed: 'He always handled his paintings in the same manner: I have seen several in which some details are executed with the greatest of care, while the rest seem to be painted with a house painter's brush, without the slightest heed paid to the design. However, he could not stop himself working like this and he justified himself by saying that he considered a picture finished when the master had achieved his intentions.' This account rings true. There is in any case little doubt that it was not to the wishes of his clients that Rembrandt shaped his work.

Houbraken again: 'It is said that one day he was painting a portrait so loaded with colour that one could have lifted the picture by seizing the figure by the nose. One sees in his canvases precious stones and pearl necklaces or turbans executed with so much impasto that they seem to be in relief; and it is because of this manner of painting that his pictures make such a great impression when viewed at a distance.'

The Portrait of the Syndics of the Clothmakers' Guild

Cut down, the canvas of *The Conspiracy of Julius Civilis* was little larger than the portrait of a guild meeting commissioned from Rembrandt by the clothmakers of Amsterdam. The painting was to hang in the Staalhof in

The imposing and regal portrait of *Juno* (opposite and detail below) was no doubt painted by Rembrandt to mollify the impatient collector Harmen Becker. While the face, the necklace and the right hand communicate power, the details are neglected and the left hand and arm are barely sketched in.

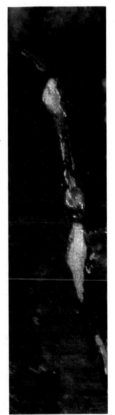

Staalstraat, the guild headquarters. It shows five men in black hats grouped round a table covered with a carpet (with a secretary in the background). The focus of attention is an open book, one man's hand poised to turn the page. Perhaps they are checking accounts? Rembrandt has caught them at a moment when they have been interrupted. They raise their eyes, turn their heads. Someone enters. *The Syndics* look at him – or at us, looking at the painting. They dominate. Their imperceptibly lowered gaze and the perspective from which the table is presented imply that the picture is at a good height, viewers have to raise their eyes to look at the men who are gathered there.

It is not certain whether the group consists of Jan Bitter, Cornelis Egbertsz Cover, Willem van Renevelt, Servaes del Court and Jan Jansz Arentburg, who in the years 1661 and 1662 were in charge of cloth control; or of Willem van Doyenburg, Volkert Janszoon, Jacob van Loon, Aernout van der Mye and Joachem de Neve, responsible in the same period for checking samples. Nor does it matter. Quite apart from being a portrait of individuals, the work is a portrait of authority and power. The magistrates of Amsterdam rejected Rembrandt's *The Conspiracy of Julius Civilis* because it did not conform to the myth in their minds. *The Syndics*, painted the following year in 1662, was different: as they raised their eyes to the painting they were forced to recognize it.

A last group painting, *The Portrait of the Syndics of the Cloth-makers' Guild* (above), was for those who accepted Rembrandt's genius but feared he would not yield a good likeness. Stiff and posed, *The Guild of Wine Merchants* (left) is by Rembrandt's pupil Ferdinand Bol. The drawing (right) is a study for *The Syndics*.

Does the ageing painter still seek recognition by the bourgeoisie?

In a poem published in 1662 Jan Vos acclaimed Rembrandt as one of the most celebrated painters in Amsterdam. He was recognized as a master in all of Europe.

Rembrandt knew that his works were in the most important European collections, those of the king of England, and of Cardinal Richelieu. He had in 1661 sent a second painting to Don Antonio Ruffo in Messina, *Alexander the Great*, for which he was paid 500 guilders. Having in

1660 received a letter from Guercino, in which he described Rembrandt as a virtuoso on the strength of a few prints he had seen, Ruffo commissioned another painting from him: a *Homer*.

Was it because Ruffo's commissions accorded well with his own ideas (he had painted *Aristotle Contemplating the Bust of Homer* for Ruffo in 1653) that Rembrandt was willing to heed his criticisms? When Ruffo objected to the way four pieces of canvas had been sewn together, Rembrandt painted a second portrait of Alexander and sent it to Sicily. And when Ruffo found the work unfinished, he happily did more work on it and returned it to Sicily.

The death of Rembrandt's second companion

The proceeds of his work for the Sicilian collector did not solve Rembrandt's financial problems. On 27 October 1662 he was forced to sell Saskia's tomb in the Oudekerk. The one he bought in the Westerkerk, at the end of the Rozengracht, was no doubt cheaper. He had to borrow money.

The will Hendrickje had made on 7 August 1661 when she was ill, giving Rembrandt a life interest in her estate, of which their daughter Cornelia was the legal heiress, could not have served him as security. It testified, however, to the close relationship between them.

Like Saskia in a comparable deed drawn up by a notary in 1642, Hendrickje is termed *juffrouw* (madam), and *huisvrouw* (spouse). Did Rembrandt and Hendrickje marry? While it is possible, there is no proof. For years Rembrandt had refused to do so in order not to forfeit his claims on Saskia's estate. Then debt and bankruptcy won the day. What Hendrickje left when she died at the end of July 1663 was derisory. She was buried at the Westerkerk, where Saskia's remains now lay.

Rembrandt painted *Aristotle Contemplating the Bust of Homer* (below) in 1653 for a rich Sicilian collector who had commissioned a portrait of 'a philosopher'. Aristotle, poet and philosopher, had the added virtue in Rembrandt's eyes of being a warrior, since he was the tutor and friend of Alexander the Great. Adorned by a medallion of Alexander, the philosopher is shown resting his hand on the head of a bust of the blind poet Homer. The bust of Alexander on the medallion and Rembrandt's portrait of *Alexander the Great* (right), painted in 1663, were inspired by the same image of an armed and helmeted Pallas Athena.

Titus, still only twenty-one, is left to house, feed and help Rembrandt on his own

Rembrandt was driven to borrow again, twice having recourse to Harmen Becker. This dealer in precious stones and textiles was also a collector. He already owned several works by Rembrandt and was happy to lend money to destitute artists, accepting a painting as guarantee. When after some months Rembrandt thought he had settled all debts with Becker, it transpired that the latter had taken over from Lodewijk van Ludick the entitlement to repayment which he in turn had purchased from Jan Six. It was not money so much as a painting that Becker expected from Rembrandt: a *Juno*.

By spring 1664 Becker was growing impatient. The *Juno* was still unfinished. Why the delay? Possibly Rembrandt was busy with a commission from Frederick Rihel for an equestrian portrait commemorating his role in the guard of honour of William III when he entered Amsterdam in 1660. Perhaps he was painting a portrait of Titus.

At the beginning of 1665 one of his creditors, Isaac van Heertsbeeck, was obliged by law to return to Titus, as a privileged creditor, the proceeds he had received from the sale of Rembrandt's chattels. Titus received another 6952 guilders from the sale of the house in the Breestraat. He no doubt gave the money directly to his father. How else could Rembrandt have offered 1000 guilders for a painting by Hans Holbein the Younger? Rembrandt did not contemplate buying the house in which he now lived on the Rozengracht, the owner of which had recently died. But he continued to buy works of art.

On 29 December 1667 Cosimo III de' Medici, future Grand Duke of Tuscany, visits Rembrandt in his house on the Rozengracht

Filippo Corsini, who was accompanying him, recorded in his diary: 'Thursday 29 [December] early, the day was fine but cold, and the sky clouded over around five o'clock in the afternoon, since, as is typical of the

A rich merchant from Strasbourg, Frederick Rihel was one of 108 mounted guards who escorted the ten-year-old William III on his entry into the city of Amsterdam in 1660. It was this instant of glory that he wanted immortalized in the life-size portrait *Frederick Rihel on Horseback* (right). Equestrian portraits are a rarity in Dutch art. Indeed, in the case of Rembrandt, this one is unique, if *The Polish Rider* is taken to be by another hand. Rembrandt had in 1655 drawn *The Skeleton Rider*, in which he rendered both man and horse in skeletal form. To paint an equestrian portrait, however, meant to invite comparison with Titian's *Charles V* and Roman statues; hence no doubt the almost hieratic stiffness of the horse, reinforcing the rider's air of importance. Illuminated, in the background, the royal carriage and the young prince, can be glimpsed in profile.

climate, fog gathered and hung around until night, which is normally calm. His Highness, after attending Mass, went with Blaeu and Ferroni to look at paintings by various masters, among them the designer Wan Welde, Reinbrent the famous painter, Scamus who does seascapes, and others who did not have finished paintings, so that we visited private homes where we could look at their works, His Highness went and was greeted in the warmest and most respectful manner.'

What paintings would Cosimo have seen in the house of 'Reinbrent, the famous painter'? Unfinished portraits, perhaps: a thick-set old man whose fists grip the arms of an armchair; sketches for a pair of portraits of a man and a woman, he with his thumb upon a pair of gloves, hers upon the handle of a fan; and self-portraits. Cosimo certainly bought one for his collection. Cardinal Leopoldo de' Medici had early in the century started a collection of self-portraits by famous painters, modelled on existing collections of portraits of famous men. After the cardinal's death responsibility for this collection passed into the hands of the Grand Duke. How could a portrait of a 'famous painter' have been passed over?

Raphael's *Self-portrait* (below left) bears the marks of his Florentine sojourn and Leonardo's influence. On 28 October 1682 it became part of the collection of Cardinal Leopoldo de' Medici (1617–75) who wanted to create an equivalent to *De viris illustribus* in self-portraits of painters. Rubens' *Self-portrait* (below right) was given to Cosimo III de' Medici in 1713 by Johann Wilhelm von der Pfalz, Elector Palatine of the Rhine. The Grand Dukes of Tuscany continued the collection until the unification of Italy at the end of the 19th century.

What did Cosimo on his European tour and Rembrandt, who had never left his homeland, say to each other?

'He dissuaded his visitors from looking at his works close to, saying to each one: "The smell of the paint will displease you." ' Rembrandt did not give this advice (recounted by Houbraken) to Cosimo. The exchanges between the two men, being dictated by protocol, no doubt involved a rendering of homage and a paying of respects. Might Cosimo have seen the first stage of a portrait of a couple, or even the finished work, in the house in the Rozengracht? The illegible date on the canvas leaves us uncertain.

The man's left hand is laid over the shoulder of the young woman standing at his side whom he embraces (see over). His right hand, over which her own is laid, rests on her breast. Who were the models for this tender, serene and voluptuous portrait? The love of Jacob and Rachel, or Isaac and Rebecca? Was it Titus with the young woman he married on 10 February 1668, Magdalena van Loo, who was the daughter of the

The *Self-portrait* of Velazquez (below left) was bought in Spain in 1689 by Cosimo da Castiglione for the collection of the Grand Dukes of Tuscany. Velazquez, who was court painter to Philip IV, is carrying the keys of the 'Usher of the Chamber' office at his waist. The *Self-portrait* of Rembrandt (below right) was probably the one bought by Cosimo III de' Medici when he was visiting Amsterdam. Today it hangs in the Uffizi.

silversmith Jan van Loo? We can only speculate on the models for *The Jewish Bride* (a title which, like others, was not given by Rembrandt).

The painter makes himself one of the myths of antiquity

Was there in Rembrandt's studio a portrait of himself, bursting with mirth, in front of the faded portrait of a woman? The poet Jeremias de Decker claimed that Rembrandt was the 'Apelles of his time', 'excellent and universally known'. In the early 1630s Constantijn Huygens had written that Rembrandt surpassed Protogenes, Apelles and Parrhasius.

However, it was with none of these painters from antiquity, painters who were legends, models, beacons,

painters of whom nothing remained, that Rembrandt chose to identify himself. Instead he decided to associate himself with Zeuxis, because of the particular circumstances of Zeuxis' death.

Zeuxis, celebrated artist, was visited by an old woman who commissioned an Aphrodite from him. The painter accepted the commission. The old woman then demanded that she herself should be the model. At one of the sittings the painter burst out laughing on viewing the portrait and the model. And in the end he died laughing.

Many attempts have been made to identify the subject of this painting, known as *The Jewish Bride* (drawing left). Who is the woman? What mattered to Rembrandt was not his 'subject' so much as the feelings to which it gave rise. Amidst the rich colour he creates a feeling of joy

Rembrandt, worn out, bloated with gin, and full of wrinkles, contemplates his models

The demands of the models, the demands of painting.... Rembrandt laughed. It was grim laughter.

He was on his own. Alone with a fifteen-year-old daughter. 'He lived very simply, often making do at meals with a little bread and cheese or smoked herring.' (This detail comes from Arnold Houbraken who talked to a number of people who had known Rembrandt.)

and gentleness. He used a knife to apply the gold on the man's sleeve, its relief creating shadow. In places the paint is scraped and polished to give the material an almost tactile aspect, as inviting to the eye as it seems to the touch.

Titus, following his marriage to Magdalena van Loo, lived in his mother-in-law's house on the Singelgracht.

On 4 September 1668 Titus died. He was buried in the Westerkerk. On 22 March 1669 his daughter Titia was baptized, in the Nieuwe Zijdeskapel.

Rembrandt painted the group portrait of a family, and his own grief-stricken smile again and again; and *Simeon and the Child Jesus in the Temple*, which the painter Allart van Everdingen and his son Cornelis saw in Rembrandt's studio in September 1669.

Rembrandt painted *The Ruin* (below) in 1650. His *Family Group* (below left) was probably realized in the last year of his life. The drawing (opposite) is of the Westerkerk, where Rembrandt was buried. Overleaf: *Self-portrait* (1665).

On 4 October 1669 Rembrandt dies at the age of sixty-three

The pictures were turned against the wall. The mirrors were covered in black crape, as tradition dictated. On 8 October Rembrandt was buried in the Westerkerk next to Hendrickje and Titus. There was no official notice of his death. Only the church register recorded the fact: '8 October. Rembrandt van Rijn, painter, living in the Rozengracht, opposite Doolhof, coffin with six bearers; leaves two children. Costs charged: twenty guilders.'

A few days after his death an inventory of Rembrandt's effects was drawn up. It was necessary to determine what was to go to Cornelia and what to Titia, who would inherit under the terms of Rembrandt's formal agreement with Hendrickje and Titus. The inventory of the contents of the house in Sint Anthoniesdijk in the Breestraat listed 363 items. Some fifty covered the inventory of the contents of the house in the Rozengracht. Furniture, linen, crockery, paintings, drawings.... And of course curios, weapons, pieces of armour, antiques.... Ruined and forsaken, Rembrandt had not ceased to collect 'objects he thought might be of use to a painter'.

DOCUMENTS

Inventory of Rembrandt's paintings, furniture and household effects in Sint Anthoniesdijk on the Breestraat.

This is the house in which Rembrandt lived and worked, whose contents are listed here. The front was altered in the 18th century.

In the entrance hall

Paintings
1: A small piece by Ad. Brouwer, representing a pastrycook. 2: One ditto of gamblers by the same Brouwer. 3: One ditto of a woman with child by Rembrandt van Rijn. 4: A painter's studio by the same Brouwer. 5: A fancy spread of food by the same Brouwer. 6: A plaster head. 7: Two naked children in plaster. 8: A sleeping child in plaster. 9: A shabby shoe. 10: A small landscape by Rembrandt. 11: Another landscape by the same. 12: A small standing figure by the same. 13: A candlelight scene by Jan Lievens. 14: A 'St Jerome' by Rembrandt. 15: A small painting of hares by the same. 16: A small painting of a hog by the same. 17: A small landscape by Hercules Seghers. 18: A landscape by Jan Lievensz. 19: Another one by the same. 20: A small landscape by Rembrandt. 21: 'Fighting Lions' by the same. 22: A 'Moonlight Scene' by Jan Lievensz. 23: A portrait head by Rembrandt. 24: A portrait head by the same. 25: A still-life retouched by Rembrandt. 26: A 'Soldier in Armour' by the same. 27: A 'Vanitas' retouched by Rembrandt. 28: Another one with a sceptre, retouched. 29: A seascape completed by Hendrick Antonisz. 30: Four Spanish chairs with Russian leather. 31: Two chairs with black seats. 32: A step-stool made of pine.

In the antechamber

33: A painting of the Samaritan, retouched by Rembrandt. 34: A 'Rich Man' by Palma Vecchio, of which Pieter de la Tombe owns a half share. 35: A 'Shed' by Rembrandt. 36: Two greyhounds from life by the same. 37: A large 'Descent from the

Cross' by Rembrandt, with a handsome gold frame by the same. 38: A 'Raising of Lazarus' by the same. 39: A 'Courtesan Doing Her Hair,' by the same.
40: A wooded landscape by Hercules Seghers. 41: A 'Tobias' by Lastman. 42: A 'Raising of Lazarus' by Jan Lievensz. 43: A small mountain landscape by Rembrandt.
44: A small landscape by Govaert Jansz. 45: Two portrait heads by Rembrandt. 46: A grisaille by Jan Lievensz. 47: Two grisailles by Porcellis. 48: A portrait head by Rembrandt. 49: Another one by Brouwer.
50: A view from the dunes by Porcellis. 51: A smaller one of the same by the same. 52: A small [picture of a] hermit by Jan Lievensz. 53: Two small portrait heads by Lucas van Valckenburgh. 54: A 'burning camp' by the elder Bassano. 55: 'A Quacksalver', after Brouwer. 56: Two heads by Jan Pynas. 57: A perspective view by Lucas van Leyden. 58: A priest after Jan Lievensz. 59: A small study of a model by Rembrandt. 60: A small herding scene by the same. 61: A drawing by the same. 62: A 'Flagellation of Christ' by the same. 63: A grisaille by Porcellis. 64: A grisaille by Simon de Vlieger. 65: A small landscape by Rembrandt. 66: A portrait head painted from life by Rembrandt. 67: A portrait head by Raphael of Urbino. 68: Some houses from life by Rembrandt. 69: A landscape from nature by the same. 70: Some small houses by Hercules Seghers. 71: A 'Juno' by Pynas. 72: A mirror in an ebony frame. 73: An ebony frame. 74: A marble [wine] cooling bucket. 75: A walnut table with a *tournai* cloth. 76: Seven Spanish chairs with green velvet seats.

In the room behind the antechamber

77: A painting of Jephta. 78: A 'Virgin with Child' by Rembrandt. 79: A 'Crucifixion of Christ', designed by the same. 80: A 'Naked Woman' by the same. 81: A copy after Annibale Carracci. 82: Two figures in half-length by Brouwer. 83: Another copy after Annibale Caracci. 84: A small seascape by Percelles. 85: A head of an old man by van Eyck. 86: A portrait of the deceased by Abraham Vinck. 87: A 'Resurrection of the Dead' by Aertie van Leyden. 88: A sketch by Rembrandt. 89: A copy after a sketch by Rembrandt. 90: Two portrait heads from life by Rembrandt. 91: 'The Consecration of Solomon's Temple' in grisaille by the same. 92: The 'Christ's Circumcision', copy after Rembrandt. 93: Two small landscapes by Hercules Seghers. 94: A gilded frame. 95: A small oak table. 96: Four cardboard shades [or screens]. 97: An oak press. 98: Four plain chairs. 99: Four green chair cushions. 100: A copper kettle. 101: A coat-stand.

In the room behind the parlour

102: A wooded landscape by an unknown master. 103: A head of an old man by Rembrandt. 104: A large landscape by Hercules Seg[h]ers. 105: A head of a woman by Rembrandt. 106: The 'Concord of the State' by the same. 107: A 'Small Village' by Govaert Jansz. 108: A 'Small Ox' from life by Rembrandt. 109: A large picture of 'The Samaritan Woman' by Giorgione, of which a half share belongs to Pieter [de] la Tombe. 110: Three antique statues. 111: A sketch of 'Christ's Entombment' by Rembrandt. 112: A 'St Peter's Boat' by Aertie van Leijden. 113: A 'Christ's Resurrection' by Rembrandt.

114: A figure of the Virgin by Raphael of Urbino. 115: A 'Head of Christ' by Rembrandt. 116: A small winter scene by Grimmer. 117: The 'Crucifixion of Christ' by Lelio da Novellara.
118: A 'Head of Christ' by Rembrandt. 119: A small ox, by Las[t]man.
120: A 'Vanitas' retouched by Rembrandt. 121: An 'Ecce Homo' in grisaille by Rembrandt. 122: An 'Abraham's Sacrifice' by Jan Lievensz. 123: A 'Vanitas' retouched by Rembrandt. 124: A landscape, in grisaille, by Hercules Seghers.
125: 'Sunset' by Rembrandt.
126: A large mirror. 127: Six chairs with blue seats. 128: An oak table.
129: An embroidered table cloth.
130: A cedar press. 131: A cupboard of the same [wood]. 132: A bed and bolster.
133: 2 pillows. 134: 2 blankets.
135: A blue hanging. 136: A wicker chair. 137: A warming pan.

In the art chamber

138: Two terrestrial globes. 139: A small box of minerals. 140: A small column.
141: A small pewter pot.
142: A urinating child. 143: Two East Indian cups. 144: A bowl ditto [decorated] with a little Chinaman.
145: A sculpture of an empress.
146: An East Indian powder box.
147: A sculpture of the Emperor Augustus. 148: An Indian cup.
149: A sculpture of Tiberius.
150: An East Indian sewing box.
151: A head of Caius. 152: A Caligula.
153: Two porcelain cassowaries [?].
154: A Heraclitus. 155: Two porcelain figurines. 156: A Nero. 157: Two iron helmets. 158: A Japanese helmet.
159: A Croatian helmet. 160: A Roman emperor. 161: A moor['s head] cast from life. 162: A Socrates. 163: A Homer.

164: An Aristotle. 165: A burnished antique head. 166: A Faustina.
167: An iron armour and helmet.
168: An emperor Galba. 169: A ditto Otto. 170: A ditto Vitellius. 171: A ditto Vespasian. 172: A Titus Vespasian.
173: A ditto Domitian. 174: A ditto Silius Brutus. 175: 47 specimens of land and sea animals and the like.
176: 23 sea and land animals.
177: One net with two calabashes, one made of copper. 178: Eight plaster casts from life, large.

On the shelf in the back

179: A great quantity of shells, coral branches, casts from life and many other curios. 180: A figure of an antique Cupid. 181: A hand gun, a pistol.
182: An old ornamented iron shield made by Quentin the Smith. 183: An old-fashioned powder horn. 184: A Turkish powder horn. 185: A cabinet with medals. 186: A padded shield.
187: Two completely nude figures. 188: A death-mask of Prince Maurice, cast from his own face. 189: A lion and a bull modelled from life. 190: Several walking sticks. 191: A long-bow.

[Here] follow the art books [i.e. albums]

192: A book of sketches by Rembrandt.
193: A book of woodcuts by Lucas van Leyden. 194: The same with woodcuts by Wael.... 195: One ditto with copper plate engravings by Vanni and others including Barocci. 196: One ditto with copper plate engravings by Raphael of Urbino. 197: A small gilt bedstead modelled by Verhulst. 198: One ditto with copper engravings by Lucas van Leyden including duplicates and single sheets. 199: One ditto with drawings by

the leading masters of the entire world. 200: The precious book of Andrea Mantegna. 201: One ditto of large size filled with drawings and prints by many masters. 202: Another ditto of larger size with drawings and prints by various masters. 203: One ditto filled with curious drawings in miniature as well as woodcuts and engravings on copper of various [folk] costumes.

204: One ditto with prints by the elder Breughel. 205: One ditto with prints by Raphael of Urbino. 206: One ditto with very precious prints by the same.

207: One ditto filled with prints by Antonio Tempesta. 208: One ditto with copper plate engravings and woodcuts by Lucas Cranach. 209: One ditto of Annibale, Agostino and Ludovico Carracci, Guido Reni and Spagnaletto. 210: One ditto with engraved and etched figures by Antonio Tempesta.

211: One ditto, a large book of the same. 212: One ditto book, as above.

213: One ditto book with engraved copperplate prints of portraits by Goltzius and Muller.

214: One ditto with very fine impressions [of prints] by Raphael of Urbino. 215: One ditto with drawings by Ad. Brouwer. 216: One ditto, very large, with almost all the work of Titian.

217: A few rare items of pottery and of Venetian glass. 218: One antique book with a series of sketches by Rembrandt.

219: An antique book. 220: A large book filled with sketches by Rembrandt.

221: Another antique book, empty.

222: A small backgammon board.

223: An antique chair....

224: A Chinese bowl containing minerals. 225: A large lump of white coral. 226: A book filled with copper plate engravings of statues.

227: One ditto with all the works of Heemskerck. 228: A book filled with portraits, of [or by] van Dyck, Rubens and various other old masters.

229: One ditto full of landscapes by various masters. 230: One ditto full of the work of Michelangelo Buonarroti.

231: Two woven baskets.

232: One ditto with erotica by Raphael, Rosso, Annibale Carracci and Giulio Bonasone. 233: One ditto full of landscapes by various esteemed masters.

234: One ditto full of Turkish buildings by Melchior Lorck, Hendrick Coeck van Aelst and others, depicting Turkish life.

235: One East Indian basket [?] containing various prints by Rembrandt, Hollar, Cock and others.

236: A book bound in black leather with the best sketches by Rembrandt.

237: A cardboard box with prints of Schongauer, Holbein, Hans Brosamer and Israel van Meeckenem.

238: Another book with all of Rembrandt's works. 239: A book filled with drawings by Rembrandt of nude men and woman. 240: One ditto filled with drawings of all Roman buildings and views by all the most excellent masters. 241: A Chinese basket full of portrait casts. 242: An empty album.

243: One ditto as above. 244: One ditto, full of landscapes drawn by Rembrandt from nature. 245: One ditto with trial proofs by Rubens and Jacob Jordaens.

246: One ditto full of portraits by Mierevelt, Titian and others.

247: A small Chinese basket.

248: One ditto filled with prints of architecture. 249: One ditto filled with drawings by Rembrandt of animals done from life. 250: One ditto full of prints by Frans Floris, Buytewech, Goltzius and Abraham Bloemart. 251: A packet of drawings from the antique by Rembrandt. 252: 5 small books in quarto, filled with drawings by Rembrandt. 253: One ditto with

drawings of architecture.
254: 'Medea', tragedy by Jan Six.
255: 'All of Jerusalem' by Jacques Callot.
256: A book [bound] in vellum filled with landscapes drawn from nature by Rembrandt. 257: One ditto filled with figure sketches by Rembrandt.
257a: One ditto as above. 258: A small book with wooden covers with [sketches of] circular plates. 259: A small book containing views by Rembrandt.
260: One ditto with outstanding [example of] calligraphy. 261: One ditto full of drawings of statues by Rembrandt done from life. 262: One ditto as above. 263: One ditto full of sketches by Las[t]man in pen [and ink].
264: One ditto by Las[t]man in red chalk. 265: One ditto with sketches by Rembrandt done in pen [and ink].
266: One ditto as above. 267: One ditto as before. 268: Another one ditto by the same. 269: Another one ditto by the same. 270: One ditto, large, with drawings of the Tyrol by Roelant Savery drawn from nature. 271: One ditto full of drawings by various eminent masters. 272: One ditto in quarto, filled with sketches by Rembrandt. 273: The book on proportion with woodcuts by Albrecht Dürer. 274: Another engraved book [album] with prints comprising the works of Jan Lievensz and Ferdinand Bol. 275: A few packets of sketches by Rembrandt, as well as by others.
276: A stack of paper of very large size.
277: A box of prints by van Vliet after paintings by Rembrandt. 278: A cloth room divider. 279: An iron gorget. 280: A drawer in which there is a bird of paradise and six fans. 281: 15 books of various sizes. 282: A book in High German with military figures. 283: One ditto with woodcuts. 284: A 'Flavius Josephus' in High German profusely illustrated by Tobias Stimmer. 285: An

old Bible. 286: A small marble ink stand.
287: The plaster cast of Prince Maurice.

In the antechamber of the art room

288: A 'Joseph' by Aertie van Leyden.
289: 3 framed prints. 290: 'The Annunciation'. 291: A small landscape painted from nature by Rembrandt.
292: A small landscape by Hercules Seghers. 293: The 'Descent from the Cross' by Rembrandt. 294: A head, from life. 295: A death's head, painted over by Rembrandt. 296: A 'Diana Bathing', in plaster by Adam van Vianen.
297: A [study of a] model, from life, by Rembrandt. 298: Three little dogs done from life by Titus van Rijn.
299: A painted book by the same.
300: A 'Head of the Virgin' by the same.
301: A small landscape in moonlight, overpainted by Rembrandt.
302: A copy of 'Christ's Flagellation' after Rembrandt. 303: A small [picture of a] nude woman, done from life by Rembrandt. 304: A small unfinished landscape, from nature, by the same.
305: A horse, from nature, by the same.
306: A small picture by the young Hals.
307: A small [picture of a] fish, from life.
308: A bowl, modelled in plaster, with nude figures, by Adam van Vianen.
309: An old trunk. 310: 4 chairs with black leather seats. 311: A pine table.

In the small studio

312: 33 pieces of antique hand weapons and wind instruments. 313: 60 pieces of Indian hand weapons, arrows, shafts, javelins and bows. 314: 13 pieces of bamboo wind instruments. 315: 13 pieces of arrows, bows, shields, etc.
316: A large quantity of hands and heads cast from life, together with a harp and a Turkish bow. 317: 17 hands and arms,

cast from life. 318: A quantity of antlers. 319: 4 crossbows and footbows. 320: 5 antique helmets and shields. 321: 9 gourds and bottles. 322: 2 sculpted heads of Barthold Been and his wife. 323: A plaster cast of a Greek antique. 324: A statue of the Emperor Agrippa. 325: Ditto of the Emperor Aurelius. 326: A head of Christ, a study from life. 327: A satyr's head with horns. 328: An antique Sibyl. 329: An antique Laocoön. 330: A large sea plant. 331: A Vitellius. 332: A Seneca. 333: 3 or 4 antique heads of women. 334: Another 4 different heads. 335: A small [model of ?] a metal cannon. 336: A quantity of ancient textiles of various colours. 337: 7 stringed instruments. 338: Two small paintings by Rembrandt.

In the large studio

339: 20 pieces, including halberds, swords and Indian fans. 340: [A pair of] costumes for an Indian man and woman. 341: A giant's head. 342: 5 cuirasses. 343: A wooden trumpet. 344: Two Moors in a picture by Rembrandt. 345: A little child by Michelangelo Buonarroti.

On the picture rack

346: The skins of a lion and a lioness with two multicoloured coats. 347: A large picture of Danae. 348: A bittern from life, by Rembrandt.

In the small office

349: Ten pieces, small and large paintings, by Rembrandt. 350: A bedstead.

In the small kitchen

351: A pewter water jug. 352: Several pots and pans. 353: A small table. 354: A cupboard. 355: Several old chairs. 356: 2 seat cushions.

In the hallway

357: 9 white bowls. 358: 2 earthenware dishes.

Linen at the laundry

359: 3 men's shirts. 360: 6 handkerchiefs. 361: 12 napkins. 362: 3 tablecloths. 363: A few collars and cuffs.

Thus done and inventoried on 25 and 26 July 1656.

Walter L. Strauss and
Marjon van der Meulen (eds.)
The Rembrandt Documents, 1979

Rembrandt and his contemporaries

From an early stage Rembrandt's exceptional ability was recognized. In these passages we are given an insight into the reactions of a connoisseur and a pupil.

J*udas Returning the Thirty Pieces of Silver* (detail, 1629).

Constantijn Huygens, private secretary to the Stadholder, was a great admirer of Rembrandt's art. His diary, written in 1631 in Latin, contains one of the earliest and most enthusiastic descriptions of the young painter's work.

His picture of Judas repenting, who brings back to the High Priest the pieces of silver, the reward for his treason to Our Lord, can, in my opinion, stand comparison with any work of art. Let the whole of Italy attempt to compete with that picture as well as anything beautiful or admirable that has come down from the earliest times. Setting aside the many figures contained in that single canvas, I would like to draw attention to one figure – that of Judas in his despair: his face tortured by fear, in convulsions of rage, begging, craving for remission, and yet with not a gleam of hope, his hair tousled, his garments in rags, his arms distorted, his hands twisted until the blood flows, flinging himself frantically on his knees, his whole body

bent in miserable suffering – all that I would like to contrast with the elegance of our men of the world, and then even the most ignorant of all mortal men would understand, that antiquity has not produced anything comparable either in poetry or painting. For I would claim that neither Protogenes, nor Apelles, nor Parrhasius could have conceived, nor would be able to conceive even if they could come back to life, such a wealth of special and general features – I tremble in writing this down! – as this Dutch son of a miller in his single figure. Praise and hail to you, my Rembrandt! Neither Troy nor the whole of Asia have brought so much high fame to Italy as Italy and Greece together have brought to the Netherlands – in the person of a young Dutchman who has scarcely ever been beyond the bounds of his home town, let alone his country.

Diary of Constantijn Huygens
Quoted in Richard Friedenthal
Letters of the Great Artists
Translated by Daphne Woodward, 1963

One of Rembrandt's pupils, the painter
Bernhardt Keil, reveals the master's
working methods in an account given
by Filippo Baldinucci in 1686.

This painter, different in his mental make-up from other people as regards self-control, was also most extravagant in his style of painting and evolved for himself a manner which may be called entirely his own, that is, without contour or limitation by means of inner and outer lines, but entirely consisting of violent and repeated strokes, with great strength of darks after his own fashion, but without any profound darks. And that which is almost impossible to understand is this: how, painting by means of these strokes, he worked so slowly, and completed his things with a tardiness and toil never equalled by anybody. He could have painted a great number of portraits, owing to the great prestige which in those parts had been gained by his colouring, to which his drawing did not, however, come up; but after it had become commonly known that whoever wanted to be portrayed by him had to sit to him for some two or three months, there were few who came forward. The cause of his slowness was that, immediately after the first work had dried, he took it up again, repainting it with bigger or smaller strokes, so that at times the pigment in a given place was raised more than half the thickness of a finger. Hence it may be said of him that he always toiled without rest, painted much, and completed very few pictures. Nevertheless, he always managed to retain such an esteem that a drawing by him, in which little or nothing could be seen, was sold by auction for 30 scudi, as is told by Bernhardt Keil of Denmark, the much-praised painter now working in Rome. This extravagance of manner was entirely consistent with Rembrandt's mode of living, since he was a most temperamental man and despised everyone. The ugly and plebeian face by which he was ill-favoured was accompanied by untidy and dirty clothes, since it was his custom, when working, to wipe his brushes on himself, and to do other things of a similar nature. When he worked he would not have granted an audience to the first monarch in the world, who would have had to return and return again until he had found him no longer engaged upon that work.

Filippo Baldinucci
Quoted in *Rembrandt: Selected Paintings*
Introduction and notes by
Tancred Borenius, 1942

Two painters look at Rembrandt

Artists continued over the centuries to look on Rembrandt as a master. His work was a point of reference, a challenge, an enigma. It was his fellow painters who 'talked painting' and defined the plasticity of his art.

I*nterior of a Gallery of Pictures and Objets d'art* by Cornelis de Brellieur.

The good use of exaggeration: Eugène Delacroix observes the work of Rembrandt

6 June 1851

Although it is necessary to take account of all the parts of the figure, so as not to misrepresent the proportions that clothing may hide, I do not think one should subscribe exclusively to this method, as he always seems scrupulously to have done, to judge by the studies by him which remain. I am very sure that if Rembrandt had confined himself to this studio practice he would not have achieved either the theatrical power or the mastery of effects that make his pictures such true renderings of nature. Perhaps Rembrandt will prove in the long run to be a far greater painter than Raphael.

I write this blasphemy, calculated to horrify every right-thinking student of painting, without wanting to make an issue of it; it is only that the more I progress through life, the more I am inwardly convinced that truth is what is most beautiful and most rare. What Rembrandt lacks, if you will, is the absolute elevation of Raphael.

Perhaps that elevation which Raphael has in the lines, in the majesty of each of his figures, Rembrandt has in his mysterious conception of his subjects, in the deep naturalness of their expressions and gestures. Although one may prefer the majestic emphasis of Raphael, which is perhaps suited to the grandeur of certain subjects, one can reasonably claim, without inviting the derision of men of taste, and I mean genuine and sincere taste, that the great Dutchman was more instinctively a painter than the studious pupil of Perugino.

The Storm on the Sea of Galilee (1633), the only seascape by Rembrandt.

28 April 1853

It takes a multitude of *sacrifices* to get the maximum effect in painting, and I believe I make a good many, but I can't bear it when the artist shows his hand. There are notwithstanding very fine things that have been conceived to produce an extreme effect, among them the works of Rembrandt and our native Decamps. Exaggeration is natural to them and not at all shocking in their case. I make this reflection as I look at my portrait of M. Bruyas; Rembrandt would have concentrated on the head; the hands would have been barely indicated, likewise the clothing. Without saying that I prefer the method which presents all objects to the eye according to their degree of importance – for I admire Rembrandt exceedingly – I feel that I should manage clumsily in attempting those effects. I am on the side of the Italians in this. Paul Veronese is the *ne plus ultra* of rendering, in all parts of the picture; the same is true of Rubens, and perhaps he has the advantage over the glorious Paolo when it comes to pathos, in that he knows how to draw attention to the principal object by selective exaggerations, thus intensifying the expressive force of his work. On the other hand there is something artificial in this manner, which one feels as much or perhaps even more than the sacrifices in Rembrandt's work, and the vagueness that he employs in such a marked way in the less important areas. Neither alternative satisfies me when it comes to my own case. What I want – and I believe I often encounter it – is that artifice should be barely perceptible, and that the object of interest should nonetheless be properly singled out; something which can once again only be achieved by sacrifices; however, these need to be infinitely more subtle than those found in Rembrandt's work to accord with my taste.

5 July 1854

It is really only with Rembrandt that one begins to see in pictures a harmony between the accessory features and the main subject, to my mind one of the most important things, if not the most important. On this subject one could compare the work of the famous masters.

29 July 1854

The landscapes of Titian, of Rembrandt, and of Poussin are, as a rule, in harmony with the figures. In the case of Rembrandt himself – and he carries this to perfection – the background and the figures are absolutely one. Interest is everywhere: you do not isolate any part, any more than when contemplating a beautiful scene in nature, where everything contributes to your delight....

When copying a Titian or a Rembrandt we think that we are

rendering the relationship of light and shade in the same terms as the master; we religiously reproduce the work or, rather, the ravages worked on it by time. The great men would be very painfully surprised to come upon smoky daubs instead of their works as they actually painted them.

29 October 1857

One does not generally find in French painting any of that felicitous neglect of detail which has the merit of drawing the attention to the parts that deserve it. The Flemish excel in this, not to mention Rembrandt, in whom this feature is as much the product of calculation as of instinct, his capricious etching needle committing itself to no more than a superficial rendering, even in the essential parts. One notices in the works of the Dutch and the Flemish, in their paintings as in their engravings, an ease of execution, an artful concealment of sacrifices that captures the imagination.

Eugène Delacroix
Journal, 1822–63

Contemplating Rembrandt, for whom light was more a matter of emphasis than of colour, Vincent van Gogh asked himself if black and white were 'forbidden fruit'.

18 September 1877

So, having some leisure, I could carry out an old plan to go to see the etchings by Rembrandt in the Trippenhuis; I went there this morning, and am glad I did. While there, I thought, Couldn't Theo and I see them together someday? Think about whether you could spare a day or two for such things. How would a man like Father, who so often goes long distances, even in the night with a lantern, to visit a sick or dying man, to

speak with him about One whose word is a light even in the night of suffering and agony – how would he feel about Rembrandt's etchings, for instance, 'The Flight into Egypt in the Night' or the 'Burial of Jesus'? The collection in the Trippenhuis is splendid....

Blessed twilight, when two or three are

T*he Entombment,* an etching of 1654.

gathered in His name and He is in the midst of them, and blessed is he who knows these things and follows them, too.

Rembrandt knew that, for from the rich treasure of his heart he produced, among other things, that drawing in sepia, charcoal, ink, etc., which is in the British Museum representing the house in Bethany. In that room twilight has fallen; the figure of our Lord, noble and impressive, stands out serious and dark against the window, which the evening twilight is filtering through. At Jesus' feet sits Mary who has chosen the good part, which shall not be taken away from her; Martha is in the room busy with something or other – if I remember correctly, she is stirring the fire, or something like that. I hope I forget neither that drawing nor what it seems to say to me: 'I am the light of the world: he that followeth me shall not walk in darkness, but shall have the light of life.'

30 October 1877
I cannot sit up so late in the evening any more – uncle has strictly forbidden it. Still, I keep in mind the phrase under the etching by Rembrandt, 'In medio noctis vim suam lux exerit' (in the middle of the night, the light diffuses its strength), and I keep a small gaslight burning low all night; 'in medio noctis' I often lie looking at it, planning my work for the next day and thinking of how to arrange my studies best.

I hope to light the fire early in the morning this winter, the winter mornings have something peculiar about them.

October 1885
'The Syndics' [see pp. 116–7] is perfect, is the most beautiful Rembrandt; but 'The Jewish Bride' [above] – not ranked so high – what an intimate, what an infinitely sympathetic picture it is, painted d'une main de feu. You see, in 'The Syndics' Rembrandt is true to nature, though *even there*, and always, he soars aloft, to the very highest height, the infinite; but Rembrandt could do more than that – if he did not have to be *literally* true, as in a portrait, when he was free to *idealize*, to be poet, that means Creator. That's what he is in 'The Jewish Bride'. How Delacroix would have understood that picture. What a noble sentiment, infinitely deep. 'Il faut

T*he Jewish Bride* (detail, *c.* 1668).

être mort plusieurs fois pour peindre ainsi' [One must have died several times to paint like that], how true it is here. As to the pictures by Frans Hals – he always remains on *earth* – one can speak about them. Rembrandt is so deeply mysterious that he says things for which there are no words in any language. Rembrandt is truly called *magician* ... that's not an easy calling.

October 1885
I have especially admired the hands by Rembrandt and Hals, certain hands in 'The Syndics', even in 'The Jewish Bride' and in Frans Hals, hands that lived, but were not finished in the sense they demand nowadays.

October 1885
The fragment, Rembrandt's 'Lesson in Anatomy', yes, I was absolutely staggered by that too. Do you remember those flesh colours – it is – *de la terre* – especially the feet [see p. 99].

S*askia as Flora* (1635).

You know, Frans Hals' flesh colours are also earthy, used here in the sense that you know. Often at least. Sometimes, I almost dare say always, there is also a relation of contrast between the tone of the costume and the tone of the face....

Of Millet, Rembrandt and, for instance, Israels, it has truly been said that they are more harmonists than colourists.

But tell me, *black* and *white*, may they be used or may they not, are they forbidden fruit?

I don't think so....

December 1885

Yesterday I saw a large photograph of a Rembrandt which I did not know, and which struck me tremendously; it was a woman's head, the light fell on the bust, neck, chin and the tip of the nose – the lower jaw.

The forehead and eyes in the shadow of a large hat, with probably red feathers. Probably also red or yellow in the low-necked jacket. A dark background. The expression, a mysterious smile like that of Rembrandt himself in his self-portrait in which Saskia is sitting on his knee and he has a glass of wine in his hand [see p. 60].

These days my thoughts are full of Rembrandt and Hals all the time, not because I see so many of their pictures, but because among the people here I see so many types that remind me of that time.

I still go often to those popular balls, to see the heads of the women and the heads of the sailors and soldiers. One pays the entrance fee of 20 or 30 centimes, and drinks a glass of beer, for they drink very little spirits, and one can amuse oneself a whole evening, at least I do, by watching these people enjoy themselves.

To paint a great deal from the model – that is what I must do, and it is the only thing that seriously helps to make progress....

I know that you are sufficiently convinced of the importance of being *true* so that I can speak out freely to you.

If I paint peasant women, I want them to be peasant women; for the same reason, if I paint harlots I want a harlot-like expression.

That was why a certain harlot's head by Rembrandt struck me so enormously. Because he had caught so infinitely beautifully that mysterious smile, with a gravity such as only he possesses, the

magician of magicians.

This is a new thing for me, and it is essentially what I want.

May 1890

I am perhaps going to try to work from Rembrandt, I have especially an idea for doing the 'Man at Prayer' in the scale of colour from light yellow to violet.

The Complete Letters of Vincent van Gogh
Translated by J. van Goch-Bonger and
C. de Dood, 1958

David in Prayer, an etching of 1652.

"It is with night that he makes day."

Eugène Fromentin, the painter of Algeria, was also an influential art critic. In The Masters of Past Time, *first published in 1876, he devotes several chapters to Rembrandt and* The Night Watch *(below).*

The Night Watch in the Trippenhuis

I shall surprise no one when I say that *The Night Watch* has no charm whatsoever, and this fact is without parallel among beautiful works of pictorial art. It astonishes and disconcerts, it obtrudes itself upon us, but it utterly lacks the primary insinuating attraction to win us over, and at first sight it nearly always displeases. First of all it offends that logic and habitual rectitude of the eye which likes distinct forms, lucid ideas, clearly formulated objectives; something warns you that the imagination, like the reason, will be only half-satisfied, and that the most easily persuaded of minds will succumb only in the long run, and will not yield without argument. There are several reasons for this and not all are the

fault of the picture – there is the light, which is detestable; the dark wooden frame, which makes the painting seem lost and fails to bring out either its significant points, its bronze tone, or its power, while causing it to look even more smoky than it really is; last and most important, there are the restrictions of space, which prevent the canvas being hung at a suitable height, and, contrary to all the most elementary laws of perspective, force you to view it close-up and on a level....

An enigmatic work?

You will be aware that *The Night Watch* is regarded, rightly or wrongly, as a virtually incomprehensible work, and this is one of the reasons for its great prestige. Perhaps it would have caused far less commotion in the world if, for the last two centuries, people had not continued the habit of looking for its meaning instead of examining its merits and persisted in the folly of viewing it as a picture which was above all else enigmatic.

Considering the work in its literal sense, what we know of the subject seems to me sufficient. First, we know the names and the occupations of the personages, for the painter carefully wrote them on a cartouche at the bottom of the picture; and this shows that, while the painter's fantasy has transfigured many things, the basic elements at any rate were taken from real life. We do not know the purpose for which these people are coming out with their weapons, whether they are going to shooting practice, on parade, or somewhere else; but as this is not a very profound mystery, I am sure that if Rembrandt failed to be more explicit, it was because he did not want or did not know how to be more explicit, which paves the way to

a whole series of hypothetical explanations ranging from want of ability to deliberate reticence. As to the question about the time of day – the most disputed of all and also the only one that could have been settled at the outset – it really does not require an appreciation of the way the outstretched hand of the captain throws its shadow on the flap of a coat. It is enough to remember that Rembrandt always handled light in this way, that nocturnal darkness is habitual in his work, that shadow is his normal poetic idiom, his usual means of dramatic expression, and that in his portraits, in his interiors, in his rendering of legends and stories, in his landscapes, in his etchings, as in his paintings, it is with night that he makes day....

The scene is indeterminate

It is generally acknowledged that the composition is not the principal merit of the work. The painter had not chosen the subject, and the way in which he set out to treat it did not leave scope for any great spontaneity or great lucidity in the initial realization. As a result, the scene is indeterminate, the action almost non-existent, and the focus of interest therefore very divided. An inherent defect in the basic idea, a sort of irresolution in the way it was conceived, arranged and put into effect is apparent from the beginning. Some people walking, others coming to a halt, one priming his musket, another loading it, yet another firing, a drummer who shows his face as he beats his instrument, a somewhat theatrical standard-bearer, in short, a crowd of figures fixed in the immobility proper to portraits; and these, if I am not mistaken, are the only striking features of the picture when it comes to movement....

The figures out of proportion

So there is no truth and little pictorial invention in the overall composition. Do the individual figures fare any better? I fail to see any which could be picked out as a choice piece of work.

What immediately strikes the eye is that there are disproportions between the figures without apparent reason, and in each case inadequacies and what one could call an anxiety to endow them with character which lacks any justification. The captain [the figure at the centre front of the picture] is too tall and the lieutenant too short, not only when viewed next to Captain Cocq, whose size overwhelms him, but in relation to the auxiliary figures, whose height or breadth make this undersized young man look like a child with a premature moustache. Assessing them all as portraits, they can hardly be called successful, being dubious as likenesses, and unattractive as physiognomies, which is surprising in a portrait-painter who in 1642 had demonstrated his skill....

A creature half woman, half fire-fly

There remains an episodic figure which has up till now baffled all conjecture, because it seems to personify in its traits, its dress, its strange brilliance, and its scant bearing on the subject, the magic, the romantic meaning, or, if you like, the alternative meaning of the picture. I mean the little person with the look of a witch, childish yet very old, with comet-like headdress and ornamented tresses, who glides, we scarcely understand why, among the legs of the guards, and who – a thing no less inexplicable – wears suspended from the waist a white cock, which could at a pinch be mistaken for a purse.

Whatever its reason for mixing with the assembly, this little figure seems to have nothing human about it at all. It is colourless, almost shapeless. Its age is uncertain because its traits are indefinable. Its appearance is that of a doll and its gait automatic. It has the mien of a beggar, and something like diamonds all over its body, the air of a little queen, with garments that look like rags.... She glimmers like pale fire, uncertain, flickering. The more closely one examines her, the less one can seize the subtle lines that somehow define her incorporeal existence. We come to see in her nothing but a form of remarkably strange phosphorescence which is not the natural light of reality, nor yet the ordinary brilliancy of a well-calculated artist's palette, and which adds one more element of witchery to the strangeness of the physiognomy. Note that in the place she occupies in one of the dark corners of the canvas, rather low, in the middle distance, between a man in dark red and the captain dressed in black, this eccentric light is all the more effective for the fact it is in startling contrast to its surroundings; and that, without careful safeguards, this explosion of accidental light could of itself have disorganized the whole picture....

Rembrandt the colourist

The only points on which opinion is unanimous, particularly nowadays, are the colouring of the picture, which is described as 'dazzling', 'blinding', 'unheard-of' (you will agree that words of this nature seem calculated to make one disregard them), and the execution, which is generally agreed to be masterly. The question becomes very delicate....

Reduced to the simplest of terms, the issue is as follows: to choose colours beautiful in themselves, and secondarily, to combine them in beautiful, skilful, and exact relationship. I will add that the

At her waist this mysterious small female figure bears various symbols of archery.

colours may be deep or light, of rich tint or neutral, in other words duller; 'bold', in other words nearer the *original colour* of the objects; or graded and 'broken', to use a technical term, and lastly, of diverse value (I have told you elsewhere what is meant by that) – all this is a matter of temperament, of preference, and also of suitability....

There is no abstract light

Does Rembrandt work in this way? You have only to look at *The Night Watch* to observe the contrary.

Apart from one or two bold colours, two reds and a dark violet, apart from one or two sparks of blue, you can see nothing in this colourless and violent canvas which resembles the palette and the ordinary method of any of the established colourists. The heads have the semblance rather than the colouring of

life. They are red, vinous or pale, yet they do not have the realistic pallor that Velazquez gives his faces, nor the sanguine, yellowish, greyish, or purple shades that Frans Hals so delicately sets against each other when he wants to portray the temperaments of his figures. In the clothes, the headdresses, the very various items of apparel, the colour is no more accurate or expressive than is, as I have said, the form itself. When a red is featured, it is not a very subtle red and it depicts silk, cloth, or satin indiscriminately. The guardsman loading his musket is dressed in red from head to foot, from his felt hat to his shoes. Do you perceive that the physiognomic peculiarities of this red, its nature and substance, which a true colourist would never have failed to seize, has only for a moment engaged Rembrandt's attention? This red is said to be admirably logical in its light and in its shade. In truth, I don't think that anyone, however unpractised in manipulating tonal qualities, could hold such an opinion – and I don't suppose that either Velazquez or Veronese, Titian or Giorgione, to say nothing of Rubens, would have accepted the way it is composed and laid on. I challenge anyone to tell me how the lieutenant is dressed, or the colour of his costume. Is it white tinted with yellow? Is it a yellow so pale as to seem almost white? The truth is that as this person had to convey the central light of the picture, Rembrandt clothed him in light – very skilfully in terms of brilliance, very carelessly in terms of colour.

Now, and this is where Rembrandt begins to betray himself as a colourist, there is no abstract light. Light in itself is nothing: it is the product of colours variously illumined and variously radiating, according to the nature of the ray that they reflect or absorb. One very

This watercolour copy of *The Night Watch* made in 1650 in Captain Cocq's album shows the painting before it was cut down.

dark tint may be extraordinarily luminous; another very light one may on the other hand not be so at all. Every student knows that. To colourists, then, light depends exclusively on the choice of colours used to render it and is so closely bound up with the tone that we can truly say that for them light and colour are one. In *The Night Watch* there is nothing like this. The tone disappears in the light, just as it disappears in the shade. The shade is blackish, the light whitish. Everything is brightened or darkened, everything radiates or is obscured by an oscillating effacement of the colouring principle....

Chiaroscuro

I come at last to the undeniable interest of the picture, to Rembrandt's great impetus in a new direction: I am referring to the application on a grand scale of his own particular way of seeing, which has been called chiaroscuro....

No one used it so continuously and ingeniously. It is the mysterious form *par excellence*, the most shrouded, the most elliptical, the most suggestive, the most capable of surprise to exist in the pictorial vocabulary of artists. For this reason it is, above all others, the medium of intimate feelings and ideas. It is light, vaporous, veiled, discreet; it lends its charm to elusive things, incites curiosity, adds grace to intellectual speculation. It partakes of feelings, emotions, uncertainty, the indefinite and the infinite, dreams and the ideal. And this is why it is, why it had to be, the natural poetic framework in which Rembrandt's genius constantly operated. Rembrandt's work, then, in all its inwardness and truth, can fittingly be studied in this, the usual form of his thought. And if, instead of skimming over the surface, I were to plumb the depths of this vast subject, you would see his whole psychological being materialize from the mists of the chiaroscuro; however, I shall say only what I need to say, and Rembrandt will emerge no less clearly, I hope....

The consequences of this way of seeing, feeling and rendering the elements of actual life are easily imagined. The world has a changed appearance. Defining lines are attenuated or effaced, colours are volatilized. The modelling, no longer confined by a rigid contour, becomes less definite in its stroke, more undulating in its surfaces, and when carried out by a practised and sensitive hand it is at its most life-like and convincing, for it holds a thousand artifices which give it what one could call a double life – one that springs from nature and another that has its source in the conveying of emotion. In summary, there are ways of giving a canvas depth and distance, of bringing it close, of dissimulating, of rendering apparent, and of burying the true in the imaginary: this is *art*, or more precisely, *the art of chiaroscuro*.

The light of visions

Rembrandt's whole career, then, is shaped by a constant objective: to paint only with the aid of light, to draw only with light. And all the varied criticisms that have been made of his works, beautiful or flawed, doubtful or incontestable, may be turned into one simple question: should he or should he not have attached so exclusive an importance to light? Did the subject demand it, admit of it or exclude it? If the first, it grows out of the spirit of the work; it cannot help but be admirable. If the second, the outcome is uncertain, and the work is nearly always questionable or ill conceived....

Explained in terms of the painter's tendency to portray a subject only by the lightness and darkness of things, *The Night Watch* holds, so to speak, no further secrets. All that could make us hesitate has been explained away. The qualities are now clear, the errors understandable. The problems that seem to beset him as a craftsman when he

T*he Night Watch* (detail) in 1975, during the restoration that removed the 'night'.

executes, as a draughtsman when he constructs, as a painter when he colours, and as a *costumier* when he chooses the clothes, the want of consistency in the tone, the ambiguities inherent in the structure, the uncertainty of the hour, the strangeness of the figures, their fulgent appearance even in the deepest shadows – all this seems to be the accidental result of an effect conceived, unnecessarily, in defiance of all verisimilitude and pursued in spite of all logic, an effect whose sole purpose was this: to illuminate a real scene by a light that was unreal; to endow a historical event with the ideal character of a vision.

Eugène Fromentin
The Masters of Past Time, 1876

Writers on Rembrandt

Rembrandt has inspired poetic reflection as few painters before or since. The ambiguity and power of his work strike a chord with partisans both of the sacred and of the profane – different expressions of the same disquiet.

J *an Cornelisz Sylvius, Preacher: Posthumous Portrait*, an etching of 1646.

Paul Claudel: the sacrament of light

It was a milestone in the history of art when painting ceased to have a ceremonial or decorative role and began, in complete freedom, simply to look at reality and build up a repertoire of signs and symbols whose lines and colours could be combined together to yield a meaning. The Dutch artist was no longer a will that carried out a preconceived plan to which method and movement were subordinated, he was an eye that selected and grasped, he was a mirror that painted; everything he did followed from a *reflection*, from an expert exposure of the plate to the lens; all the figures that he gave us seemed to have come back from a voyage to the land of the looking glass. The gradation of shadows, the administration of a scale of values around the focal centre, the dilution or precision of detail, corresponding to the intensity and concentration of attention, the spot of luminosity that shapes the whole in relation to itself and strangely gives rise to all kinds of scintillating effects, gradations, reflections and echoes, the importance given to emptiness and to space itself, all the silence released by an object that ensnares the eye, all this, was not invented or practised by Rembrandt alone. He was not the first nor the only one who knew how to give a canvas soul by lighting it, if I may put it thus, from behind and who knew how to marry light to the gaze, a gaze that gave being to a face by illuminating it. But where others tested a process hesitantly, he applied it with the wholeheartedness and authority of a master. All those portraits around us are not records of human life studied and elaborated with the application of a historian or a moralist. Those men, those women, have made acquaintance with the night, they come back to us not so much repulsed as stopped by a thicker medium. Bathed in a light taken from memory, they have reached self-awareness. They come forward and stir an echo there where in the artist's heart and in the deepest entrails of the earth the forces of creation and reproduction lie dormant. Along the route to extinction they have made a U-turn. They have achieved a permanence that our frail mind gropingly tries to realize. Stamped with personality, they give new life to the effigy by isolating it, an image of God, worked by circumstance and character, which lay buried in the everyday.

Hence comes the wholly special atmosphere emitted by Rembrandt's pictures and etchings, the sense of dream, of something somnolent, confined and taciturn, a sort of corruption of the night, a sort of mental acidity at grips with the shadows which under our eyes indefinitely continues its corroding activity. The art of the great Dutchman is no longer a hearty affirmation of the here and now, a burst of the imagination in the realm of the actual, a feast for our senses, the perpetuation of a moment of joy and colour. It is no longer a present on which to gaze, it is an invitation to remember. One has the impression that the painter accompanies each of his models' gestures, each of their attitudes, each of their interactions with the group, in his retrospective voyage beyond the surface and the here and now, a voyage which is indefinitely prolonged and which reaches its end less in the outlines than in the reverberations. The stimulus has stirred recollection, and recollection, surfacing in its turn, successively disturbs the superimposed layers of memory, summons other related images....

But never in front of a picture by Rembrandt does one have a sense of the

F*aust in his Study*, an etching of 1652.

permanent and definitive: it is a precarious creation, a phenomenon, a miraculous return to the past: the curtain raised for an instant is poised to fall back, the reflection fades away, the light in shifting by a margin extinguishes the marvel, the visitor who a moment ago was there has disappeared, we hardly had the time to recognize him *in the instant of breaking bread*, or, if he is still there, by this special insistence, in this magic apparition, one could say rather that he lives on. There is something here comparable to the phenomenon of the tide of which I spoke earlier, to that alternative life that animates Holland, to a fullness so total one feels that on all sides it is already preparing for the ebb. But in Rembrandt it is not a matter of water swelling our tissues and penetrating our substance. It is a matter of light, which for him is like sap, which both sustains thought and emanates from it. How he loved light! How he understood its play and its purposes, the screens which open and close on all sides of the sky, the special slant of the sunbeam that visits, crosses, investigates our inner dwelling and our powers of thought! The Egyptians and the Greeks in a world of enduring stone and intellectual thought raised naked, flowing forms, a conversation of gods remote and sacred. Rembrandt, however, is the master of the ray of light, of the gaze and all that comes to life and speech beneath the gaze, which illuminates less than it patiently coaxes figures and objects to a corresponding life....

We have covered the prodigious gallery at a pace both hesitant and rapid and now we have arrived in the central hall which is solely occupied and filled by the huge exhibit known as *The Night Watch*. It is this, across Holland and in the middle of Amsterdam, in the middle of all the painting of the Golden Age, which is touched by its glory, that I had promised myself, a good while ago, after reading the tantalizing book by Fromentin, to visit.

Immediately, as soon as one reopens one's eyes, as soon as one recovers from the soft shock of this gold amassed and distilled in the deepest reaches of the spirit, of this light that is like a purified and concentrated element, like visible thought, of this form of psychological blow, what strikes one is the composition. The two principal figures, one the Dominator, in black with a red sash and the other – the other, how to describe his attire? – who trail behind them the rest of the group, but their feet are actually on the edge of the frame! One step more – one sees that the veteran's gesture is urging his luminous companion to take it – and from the dark gateway in the rear through which they emerged they would pass into the realm

of the invisible. But what about all those other people standing by behind them, it is not for nothing they have armed themselves, brandishing all those strange weapons, will they not also start to advance? Yes indeed! From front to rear the painter has laid down all the gradations and all the nuances of movement getting under way, we even feel ourselves imitating the posture the first leg assumes when the other is already bending in readiness to advance! The flag is unfurled, the drum rolls or rather is about to roll, it even seems to me that I hear the report of a gun.

Paul Claudel
Dutch Painting, 1935

The Blindness of Tobit (detail), an etching of 1651.

The Emperor Timur on the Throne (c. 1635), a drawing after an Indian miniature.

Jean Genet: display, decrepitude and goodness

A great goodness. And I use this word to move quickly. His last portrait seems to say this: 'My intelligence is such that even wild animals will recognize my goodness.' The moral sense that drove him was not a vain quest for spiritual improvement, it was exacted by his work, or rather bound up with it. We know this because, by a chance almost unique in the history of art, a painter, who posed in front of the mirror with an almost narcissistic readiness, has left us, in parallel with his work, a series of self-portraits in which we can read the evolution of his method and the action of this evolution on the man. Or is it the other way round?

In the pictures he painted before 1642 Rembrandt appeared enamoured of display, but a display that went no further than the scene represented. The sumptuousness – in oriental portraits, biblical scenes – lay in the richness of the decors, the accessories; Jeremiah wears a very pretty robe, he rests his foot on a rich carpet, the vases on the rock are of gold, it is visible. One senses Rembrandt happy to invent or portray a conventional richness, and likewise happy to paint the extravagant *Saskia as Flora* [see pp. 58 and 142], or himself with Saskia on his knees, magnificently dressed, raising his glass [see p. 60]. He had of course from his youth painted those of lowly status – often decking them out in glorious rags – and it seemed that while he dreamt of splendour he at the same time had a predilection for the faces of the humble. With rare exceptions the sensuality that touched his brush when he painted a textile, for example, retreated when he approached a face. Even in his youth he preferred faces ravaged by age....

It has been written: Rembrandt, unlike for example Hals, was not skilled at getting a likeness in his portraits; in other words at seeing the difference between one man and another. If he did not see it, was it perhaps because it did not exist? His portraits in fact rarely convey a trait of the sitter's character: the man who is there is not, *a priori*, either weak, or cowardly, or tall, or short, or good, or wicked: he is capable, at any point, of being these things. But never is the trait of character apparently preordained. Never, as in Frans Hals, a sparkling

This etching of a *Beggar Seated on a Bank* (detail, 1630) is a self-portrait.

but fugitive humour: it is a possibility nonetheless, like everything else.

Except for Titus – who was his son – smiling, not one of his faces is serene. All seem burdened by a drama, laden. The figures, nearly always, in their grouped and concentrated attitudes, suggest a tornado in a moment's respite. They carry a weighty destiny, which they precisely evaluate, and which from one moment to the next they will pursue to its end. While Rembrandt's own drama seems to be no other than his observation of the world. He wants to know what it is all about, in order to free himself. All his figures carry the knowledge of a wound, and seek refuge from it. Rembrandt knows he is wounded, but he wants to be cured. Hence the impression of vulnerability when we look at his self-portraits, and the impression of confident strength when we are before his other pictures....

Rembrandt? Excepting a few swashbuckling portraits, all, from his earliest youth, reveal a troubled spirit in pursuit of a truth that evades him. The sharpness of his eye is not wholly explained by a compulsion to stare hard at the mirror. At times he even has an air almost wicked (remember that he actually paid to have a creditor put in prison!), vain (the arrogance of the ostrich plume on the velvet hat ... and the golden necklets...), but, little by little, the hardness of the countenance softened. In front of the mirror narcissistic satisfaction turned to anxiety and an impassioned, then tremulous, quest.

For some time he lived with Hendrickje and this marvellous woman (those of Titus apart, only Hendrickje's portraits seem fashioned of tenderness itself and the appreciation of the wonderful old bear) must have satisfied both his sensuality and his need for tenderness. In his last self-portraits one no longer reads psychological signs. If one cares to, one can see there the advent of something like an air of goodness. Or detachment? Whatever one wishes, here it comes to the same thing.

Towards the end of his life Rembrandt became good. So the mask or defence was withdrawn, the screen against the world presented by wickedness. Wickedness, and all forms of aggression, and all that we call traits of character, our humours, our desires, eroticism and vanities. Shatter the screen then to bring the world closer! But this goodness – or if one prefers detachment – was not something he had sought in order to obey a moral or religious rule (it is only, if ever, in an artist's moments of abandon that he can have faith) or to acquire a few virtues. If he had tested in the flames what one can term his characteristics, it was to have a purer vision of the world and make a truer work with it. I imagine that he ultimately did not care whether he was good or wicked, bad-tempered or patient, grasping or generous.... His task was to be but an eye and a hand. In addition, following this same egoistic path, he had to earn – what a word – the kind of purity so manifest in his last portrait as to be almost wounding. But it was clearly by the narrow path of painting that he attained it....

Around the years 1666 to 1669 there must have been in Amsterdam something other than the paintings of an old crook (if the story of the repossessed etching plates is true) and the city. There was what remained of a person reduced to extremity, almost completely extinguished, going from bed to easel, from easel to lavatory – where he continued to do rough sketches with his dirty fingernails – and what remained

was scarcely more than a cruel goodness, not far removed from imbecility. A furrowed hand that held brushes soaked in red and brown, an eye resting on objects, nothing but this, and the intelligence that linked the eye to the world was without hope.

In his last self-portrait he is quietly having a laugh. Quietly. He knows everything a painter can learn. And most of all this (well, perhaps?), that the painter is wholly concentrated in the eye that goes from the object to the canvas, and above all in the gesture of the hand that goes from the little pool of colour to the canvas.

The painter is concentrated there, in the sure and tranquil movement of the hand. Nothing but this in the world: the tranquil and trembling to and fro into which all the display, the sumptuousness, the obsessions have been transmuted. Legally there is nothing else. Thanks to a trick of signatures, everything is in the hands of Hendrickje the Admirable and in the hands of Titus. Rembrandt does not even own the canvases on which he paints.

A man has just gone by wholly taken up by his work. What else is left of him is good for the rubbish tip, but before, just before, he must again paint *The Return of the Prodigal Son*.

He died before he was tempted to play the buffoon.

Jean Genet
The Secret of Rembrandt, 1958

Art historians and Rembrandt

Holland, chiaroscuro, history, religion, mythology, 'genuine' and 'fake' are all questions that confront the art historian studying Rembrandt, whose legendary and mysterious personality precludes a single or definitive answer.

A*dam and Eve* (detail, 1638).

The central flash of life

Every Dutchman is born a painter at heart, and he cannot be otherwise. For this native gift to develop in a few minds, and be put into practice, it requires only that a moment of enthusiasm, a brief spurt of exertion set a generation or two in motion. There is not a country in the world where history and the terrain have more directly influenced the artist's rendering of life. And, whatever may have been said, Rembrandt is no exception. However, this needs to be explained. What the thousand painters of Holland take as the subject of their canvases, Rembrandt uses as the raw material of his visions. Where the others see facts, he perceives hidden connections that link his preternatural sensibility to reality and transport all that he has religiously drawn from the universal creation to the plane of a new creation. And as those among whom he lives feel only indifference to him, as his strange vision passes over the heads of the mass, he appears to be outside the mass, and even in a state of permanent antagonism to it. And yet he talks its language, it is of it that he speaks to us, and thence of he who finds there the roots of his suffering, and of his understanding, and love and hate, before mastering emotion and passion, the better to accept it as a living destiny and merge it within himself to other images of the world which he elevated together to the impartial force of his own mind.

Where then would Rembrandt have found his gold and his reds, and the silvery or reddish light where sun and spray mingle, had he not ever lived in Amsterdam, in the corner of the city that was most teeming, most squalid, near the boats unloading red rags on to the quay, rusted scrap iron, smoked herring,

View of the Bridge at Grimnesse-sluis in Amsterdam, now attributed to Rembrandt's pupil Abraham Furnerius.

gingerbread, and a sumptuous trail of scarlets and yellows on the day of the flower market? Through the ferment of the dirty streets of the Jewish quarter, where coloured cloths hung at the windows, brightening the russet shadows with a fiery glow, he made his way, along the lanes of water which lapped and reflected the ornamented façades, the painted clothes, as far as the banks of the Amstel, where, in the brilliant evenings of seaside cities, the great ships unloaded embroidered textiles, tropical fruits, exotic birds. Where then would he have acquired his taste for imaginary voyages, for glimpses of distant seas, for the magic Orient that he saw as dust dancing in a ray of sun, when it sent its beams to the depths of the cellars where dampness seeped in from the canals? And when he entered the hovels where the usurers of the ghetto weighed gold on a balance, where poor families were huddled, dressed in singed tatters, in makeshift calico rags, where in the darkness junk dealers piled iron breastplates, inlaid weapons, worked copper and leather, how could he have failed to stumble on scenes that no one attends to as soon as poverty is the norm, mothers baring their breasts to suckle their children, the old dying on straw mattresses, sores wrapped in dirty cloth and the rediscovered innocence of hunger and love?...

And meanwhile, from insouciance to unease, from the soft earthiness of the early work to the tentative, but essential, forms of his later years, it is the same driving force that dominates. One traces it from within, from form to form, in the shadow and the roving ray of light, illuminating this, concealing that, bringing a shoulder to the fore, a face, a lifted finger, an open book, a forehead, a child in a cradle. The same driving force operates choice, takes the world as an inexhaustible repository of movable symbols to be employed at will, but the will can only learn to use them as it requires, when it has understood the internal forces of which space and the masses that occupy it are the manifestation....

That which is immersed in light is the reverberation of that which is plunged in night. That which is plunged in night extends into the invisible that which is immersed in light. Thought, gaze, word, action, connect this brow, this eye, this mouth, this hand on the books, hardly noticed in the shadow, heads and bodies bent round a birth, an agony or a death. Even, and perhaps above all when his working tools were only his steel point, his copper plate, his acid, nothing but black and white, even then he handled the world like an unceasing drama that day and darkness shaped, carved, convulsed, calmed and made live and die according to his desire, his sadness, the desperate longing for eternity and the absolute that gripped his heart.

Elie Faure
History of Art, Modern Art, Vol. 4
1921–7

A Romantic view

If ever there was a man of genius in the art, it was Rembrandt. He might be said to have created a medium of his own, through which he saw all objects. He was the grossest and the least vulgar, that is to say the least commonplace in his grossness, of all men. He was the most downright, the least fastidious of the imitators of nature. He took any object, he cared not what, how mean soever in form, colour and expression, and from the light and shade which he threw upon it, it came out gorgeous from his hands. As van Dyck made one of the smallest contrasts of light and shade, and painted as if in the open air, Rembrandt used the most violent and abrupt contrasts in this

A*braham's Sacrifice* (1636).

respect, and painted his objects as if in a dungeon. His pictures may be said to be 'bright with excessive darkness'. His vision had acquired a lynx-eyed sharpness from the artificial obscurity to which he had accustomed himself. 'Mystery and silence hung upon his pencil.' Yet he could pass rapidly from one extreme to another, and dip his colours with equal success in the gloom of night, or in the blaze of the noonday sun. In surrounding different objects with a medium of imagination, solemn or dazzling, he was a true poet; in all the rest he was a mere painter, but a painter of no common stamp. The powers of his hand were equal to those of his eye; and indeed he could not have attempted the subjects he did, without an execution as masterly as his knowledge was profound. His colours are sometimes dropped in lumps on the canvas; at other times they are laid on as smooth as glass, and he not unfrequently painted with the handle of his brush. He had an eye for all objects as far as he had seen them. His history and landscapes are equally fine in their way. His landscapes we could look at for ever, though there is nothing in them. But 'they are of the earth, earthy'. It seems as if he had dug them out of nature. Every thing is so true, so real, so full of all the feelings and associations which the eye can suggest to the other senses, that we immediately take as strong an affection to them as if they were our home – the very place where we were brought up. No length of time could add to the intensity of the impression they convey. Rembrandt is the least classical and the most romantic of all painters.

William Hazlitt
'Fine Arts', *Encyclopaedia Britannica*
1817

Rembrandt the rebel

It is sometimes said that the character of Rembrandt as the rebel artist is an invention of romanticism; and it is true that during the 19th century the Rembrandt legend, especially the story of his fall from popularity and social ostracism, was given more dramatic colouring. But that the young man from Leyden saw himself as a tough and rebellious character is made perfectly clear to us in a whole series of self-portraits. The earliest of these [right], a drawing in the British Museum, is the very image of a rebel, with thick lips and strawberry nose; and the earliest etching [see p. 102 centre], done about a year later, is scarcely more refined, the truculent expression being rendered by an equally bold and truculent line. Most conclusive of all is the etching [see p. 154] where he has portrayed himself as one of his favourite beggars snarling at the prosperous, bourgeois society which was shortly to welcome him so warmly. This angry impatience with convention was a fundamental part of Rembrandt's character, and although he managed to control it during his years of prosperity, it came out strongly in his middle life and is emphasized in the three early biographies written by men who had first-hand information about him.

Kenneth Clark
Rembrandt and the Italian Renaissance
1966

Self-portrait (*c.* 1627–8).

Rembrandt Research Project

At the beginning of the 20th century the catalogue of Rembrandt's work listed over one thousand pictures. How many will it number when the team engaged in the Rembrandt Research Project have completed their investigations? Questions of authenticity have frequently arisen in Rembrandt's case. Some twenty years ago Gerson recognized only six hundred works as by Rembrandt. Critical and 'scientific' criteria are unbending. The most recent – and ongoing – study is the 'Rembrandt Research Project'. The team explains its history, objectives and methods.

Is there any need for a new catalogue of Rembrandt's paintings? It was the growing conviction that such is the case that led to the Rembrandt Research Project. There is, of course, a wealth of scholarly literature on the subject, but it is hard to avoid the impression that much of its interpretation of the artist and his work is based on a picture of his painted oeuvre that in the course of time has become corrupted. By the 1960s it was difficult for an impartial eye to accept all the works currently attributed to Rembrandt as being by a single artist....

Research naturally began from the point which studies of Rembrandt had reached in the 1960s, though without explicitly analysing the situation as it then was. As time went on, however, we became confirmed in our impression that there is scarcely any verifiable, documented continuity in respect of the attribution of Rembrandt's paintings such as there has been, to some extent, for his etchings from the 17th century onwards. Such continuity does exist for a tiny handful of paintings, but it is hard to describe these as a representative

nucleus; they leave the limits of the painted oeuvre entirely undefined....

[Already at the end of the 19th century] knowledge of the work done by pupils grew, and undoubtedly this helped to bring about a sharper picture of Rembrandt's own production. Yet only clearly identifiable works by these pupils were involved in this hiving-off; what remained formed a remarkably heterogenous and extensive oeuvre....

To Gerson, whose publications appeared when our project was in its initial stage (1968 and 1969), goes the honour of having had the courage to bring open-mindedness to his critical approach to the received image....

Given the possibility of maintaining contact with experts in other fields whenever necessary, we decided that the homogeneity of method and results would be served best by forming a team consisting of art historians only....

A second basic principle was to try to learn and describe the features – including the purely physical features – of each painting seen as an object, as fully as possible....

For the bulk of the paintings, however, examination had to be limited to what could be seen at the surface, and the interpretation of what was observed must, however usable this might be for comparative purposes, be termed an overall one. We have, for example, called the layer that shows through discontinuities or translucent patches in the paint layer simply 'the ground' without further distinction, and have referred to it as such in our descriptions. It was only at a late stage that we formed the hypothesis that this layer (usually a light, yellowish brown) is in some cases not the actual ground but rather part of the preparatory brush drawing on top of it, executed in predominantly translucent brown; while the ground proper does show through this, it is not necessarily directly visible....

The most familiar technique, and one which the art historian has known for a long time, is the X-ray photograph.... For us, the importance of X-rays came to lie mainly in understanding how the young Rembrandt set out his composition, applied the first layer of paint and worked towards completion....

Dendrochronology has opened up new perspectives for the dating of oak panels....

Physical and chemical examination of sample material from the ground and paint layers already occupies a fairly important role in the literature, but this is only seldom clearly related to what the art historian is seeking.... Without being unfair to either, we might perhaps say that the scientist arrives at his interpretation from relatively fragmentary and, of itself, unstructured information relating to the physical make-up of the work of art, while the art historian is concerned mainly with the stylistic interpretation of the picture and its execution....

In general, we have limited ourselves, in most catalogue entries, to dealing with present knowledge in iconography and, in a few cases, to making suggestions based on views gained from this. Sometimes these differ sharply from commonly held and still rather romantically tinged ideas of the meaning that Rembrandt's pictures may have held for him and his contemporaries.

Some reflections on method

We realized ... that the results of scientific examination would never be able to provide proof of whether a painting was by Rembrandt himself, by

B irds of Paradise.

one of his pupils or by a painter in his immediate circle. We did hope for firm evidence in the category of works which we believed, on stylistic grounds, might be later imitations of Rembrandt's style.... We found not only that the number of 'demonstrably later' paintings was almost negligible, but even that some of those that we had, because of stylistic features, regarded as being 18th or 19th century in origin could be proved, or virtually proved, to date from the 17th....

In our catalogue entries the reader will find no poetry. We positively mistrust poetic evocations of Rembrandtish qualities. Deeply-felt songs of praise have been written in the past about highly suspect paintings in which no one believes today. The tone in our catalogue is usually very down-to-earth.

Having set out their objectives and explained their methods, the Rembrandt Research Project team divide the works they have examined into three categories: A = a geniune Rembrandt, B = a work questionably by Rembrandt, C = a work wrongly attributed to Rembrandt.

Example of a work not accepted as by Rembrandt: C. 42 *Bust of an Old Woman* (commonly called *Rembrandt's Mother*)

Summarized opinion
An imitation [p. 162*l*], based on the etching B. 353 [p. 162*r*] which was formerly wrongly attributed to Rembrandt....

Comments
The extremely disorganized handling of paint, with strange colour accents (in the lit eyelid and elsewhere), together with the superabundance of scratchmarks that frequently fail to show form as they are intended to do, make it impossible to believe that the painting was done by Rembrandt or even within his circle.

The execution is so coarse, and there is so little suggestion of form, that it must rather be described as an extremely superficial attempt to achieve a Rembrandt-like effect. One can comment, furthermore, that neither the flat, opaque grey background nor the use of so much flat, thin grey-black devoid of modelling is imaginable in Rembrandt or his pupils....

This conclusion can be supported with two arguments. In the first place, the old woman has been painted on top of another picture which, so far as one can see from the X-ray, is laid in with a most unusual technique that must be termed inconceivable for a 17th-century Dutch painting. This first, apparently uncompleted painting was still not fully dry when the present picture was done on top of it; this can be assumed from the fissure-like nature of the irregular craquelure.

In the second place, the portrait does not, as has been generally assumed in the literature, resemble Rembrandt's etching B. 352 [p. 163*l*] of an old woman, of 1628, but rather etching B. 353

[p. 162*r*]. This latter etching has long been regarded as an imitation of B. 352 in combination with B. 354; it was attributed by A. D. de Vries Az. (in: O.H. 1, 1883, p. 294) to Samuel van Hoogstraten and by C. White and K. G. Boon (Hollst. XVIII, p. 183, no. B. 353) to Michael Lukas Leopold Willmann (Königsberg 1630 – Kloster Leubus 1706). This etching was clearly the prototype for the painting, which with one or two variations (the cast shadow of the head-shawl does not extend so far downwards) resembles it so closely that the apparently arbitrary scratchmarks on the cheek at the left and elsewhere become understandable as borrowed from the etching.

The date of no. C. 42 cannot for the moment be determined with any accuracy. Etching B. 353 provides a *terminus post quem* of shortly after 1650. Closer investigation of the type of wood used for the panel and, if possible, dendrochronological measurements might perhaps yield more precise information.

Which of these portraits is a fake? The Rembrandt Research Project questions the authenticity of the two on p. 162.

Summary

From the execution – in itself confused, and differing in brushwork and use of colour from the habits of Rembrandt and his school – from the interpretation of the underlying painting seen in the X-ray, and from the use made, as a prototype, of an etching once wrongly attributed to Rembrandt, one must conclude that no. C. 42 is an imitation. There is every reason to assume that it was not done until the second half of the 17th century at the earliest.

Selected passages from
Rembrandt Research Project
A Corpus of Rembrandt Paintings, Vol. 1
1982

Picture this

Rembrandt, in his self-portraits, was his own best biographer. Others have sought to link his various figures to his life. Joseph Heller made Rembrandt a character in a novel, which allowed him to 'invent' to complete the puzzle.

Here Rembrandt, as a character in a novel, a painter at work, is occupied with a well-timed commission, faced by his client and his model of course, and his debts and his memories, and the spirit of the philosopher he has chosen to portray: Aristotle.

Rembrandt painting Aristotle contemplating the bust of Homer was himself contemplating the bust of Homer where it stood on the red cloth covering the square table in the left foreground and wondering how much money it might fetch at the public auction of his belongings that he was already contemplating was sooner or later going to be more or less inevitable.

Aristotle could have told him it would not fetch much. The bust of Homer was a copy.

It was an authentic Hellenistic imitation of a Hellenic reproduction of a statue for which there had never been an authentic original subject....

About the money to be paid for the painting there could be no doubt. The terms had been set beforehand in correspondence between the Sicilian nobleman ordering the work and Dutch agents in Amsterdam, one of whom, probably, should be credited with proposing Rembrandt for the commission and bringing together these two figures significant in the art world of the 17th century who would never meet, whose association as patron and performer spanned more than eleven years, and between whom there would pass at least one acrimonious exchange of messages in which the purchaser complained he was cheated and the artist responded he was not.... The price of the painting was five hundred guilders.

Five hundred guilders was a good piece of money in the Netherlands back in 1653, even in Amsterdam, where the cost of living tended to be higher than elsewhere in the province of Holland and in the six other provinces making up the newly recognized and rather loosely organized federation of the United Netherlands, or the Dutch Republic.

Five hundred guilders was eight times the amount, Don Antonio Ruffo complained angrily in writing nine years later, that he would have had to pay to an Italian artist for a picture the size he had commissioned. He did not know that it was perhaps *ten* times the amount Rembrandt could then have demanded in Amsterdam, where he was past the peak of his fashionability and facing a financial catastrophe whose drastic consequences were to keep him impoverished for the rest of his life....

In 1961, the cost of the painting to the Metropolitan Museum of Art was a record $2,300,000.

For five hundred guilders in Amsterdam in 1653, a busy artisan or shopkeeper could support himself and his family rather well for a full year. A house in the city could be bought for that much....

Aristotle Contemplating the Bust of Homer (1653).

For the widower Rembrandt van Rijn, who had bought his house for thirteen thousand guilders and who had lived *very* well in the ten or eleven years in which his reputation had dimmed and the income he had grown used to had lessened, five hundred guilders was not going to be enough.

After fourteen years, he still owed more than nine thousand guilders on his house, an obligation he was to have satisfied in six. The country was at war with England, her occasional Protestant ally in her long revolution against Spain. And this time it was already clear that the Dutch were not going to win. There was plague in the city. Financial discouragement was epidemic. The economy was poor, capital was growing scarce, and the owners of the debt were insisting they be paid.

Rembrandt's house was a luxurious urban mansion of the Dutch kind in a choice residential area on one of the broadest and most fashionable avenues in the east side of the city, the St Anthoniesbreestraat. The word *breestraat*, by which the excellent thoroughfare was known in its diminutive, translates literally into 'broad street'.

It was next to a corner site amid other dwellings of similar restrained elegance in which resided a number of the city's wealthiest burghers and officials, several of whom had been his first patrons and sponsors. When Rembrandt bought it, the initial expenses had been met with money from the dowry of his wife, Saskia, combined with his own considerable earnings in the years he was extolled in Amsterdam and his career as a painter was flourishing.

Between 1632 and 1633, it is reported, young Rembrandt executed fifty paintings in a deluge of commissions he received after moving from Leiden to Amsterdam in 1631, when he was twenty-five. Fifty in two years averages out to just about one painting every two weeks.

If the figure is a lie, it is a very impressive lie, and there is no doubt that Rembrandt and Saskia, who was the orphaned daughter of a former burgomaster of Leeuwarden in Friesland, and the cousin of his esteemed art dealer in Amsterdam, had considerable social legitimacy with the city's middle class. In Holland in the 17th century, the middle class was the upper class.

Now, Rembrandt had debts that he could not meet.

Rembrandt contemplated often as he worked on Aristotle contemplating the bust of Homer that he was going to have to either sell the house or borrow from friends to finish paying for it, and he knew already that he was going to borrow.

As he added more and more black to

Aristotle's robe and put still more mixtures of black into a background of innumerable dark shadings – he enjoyed watching the way his canvases drank up black – he contemplated also that after he had borrowed from friends to finish paying for the house, he would put the house in the name of his small son, Titus, to protect it from seizure by these friends when he decided not to repay them.

He could not take more money from the legacy of Titus, who was too young to know that his father had taken any money from him at all.

Rembrandt was forty-seven, and facing ruin.

Saskia had died eleven years earlier. Of the four children born to Mr and Mrs Rembrandt van Rijn in the eight years of their marriage, Titus, the last of the four, was the only one to live longer than two months.

Aristotle contemplating Rembrandt contemplating Aristotle often imagined, when Rembrandt's face fell into a moody look of downcast introspection, similar in feeling and somber hue to the one Rembrandt was painting on him, that Rembrandt contemplating Aristotle contemplating the bust of Homer might also be contemplating in lamentation his years with Saskia. The death of a happy marriage, Aristotle knew from experience, is no small thing, nor is the death of three children.

Rembrandt lived now with a woman named Hendrickje Stoffels, who had come into his house as a maidservant and soon would be carrying his child.

Aristotle could understand that too....

Aristotle, so thorough and correct in drawing his own will, had to wonder occasionally what went on in the mind of the notary who had assisted Saskia van Uylenburgh [Ulenborch] with hers....

'Why do all your people look so sad

Self-portrait (above, 1652).

now?' inquired the tall man modeling for Aristotle.

'They worry.'

'What do they worry about?'

'Money,' said the artist.

But that kind of tremulous solemnity was absent from his own face in the domineering self-portrait of 1652 [above] on the opposite side of the attic, in which Rembrandt stood upright in his working tunic with his hands on his hips and appears defiant and invincible today to any onlooker who dares meet his eyes in the Kunsthistorisches Museum in Vienna.

Pensive torment he reserved for his paintings of others.

Joseph Heller
Picture This, 1988

FURTHER READING

GENERAL

Alpers, Svetlana. *Rembrandt's Enterprise: The Studio and the Market.* 1988

Brown, Christopher, Jan Kelch and Pieter van Thiel. *Rembrandt: The Master and his Workshop,* 2 vols. 1991

Fuchs, R. H. *Dutch Painting.* 1978

Haak, Bob. *Rembrandt: His Life, His Work, His Time.* 1969

—. *The Golden Age: Dutch Painters of the Seventeenth Century.* Trans. and ed. by E. Willems-Treeman. 1984

—. *Rembrandt Drawings.* 1984

Münz, Ludwig. *Rembrandt.* 1984

—, and Bob Haak. *Rembrandt.* 1966

Partsch, Susanna. *Rembrandt.* Trans. Terry Bond. 1981

Puppi, Lionello. *Rembrandt.* 1969

Rosenberg, Jakob. *Rembrandt: Life and Work.* 1964

Schwartz, Gary. *Rembrandt: His Life, His Paintings.* 1985

—. *Rembrandt.* 1991

Slive, Seymour. *Rembrandt and his Critics 1630–1730.* 1953

Strauss, Walter L., and Marjon van der Meulen (eds.). *The Rembrandt Documents.* 1979

White, Christopher. *Rembrandt.* 1984

—. *Rembrandt: Self-portraits.* 1982

PAINTINGS

Bredius, Abraham. *The Complete Edition of the Paintings of Rembrandt,* revised edition by Horst Gerson. 1969

Gerson, Horst. *Rembrandt Paintings.* 1968

Rembrandt Research Project. *A Corpus of Rembrandt Paintings,* 3 vols. 1982–9

DRAWINGS

Benesch, Otto. *Rembrandt as a Draughtsman.* 1960

—. *The Drawings of Rembrandt,* 6 vols. 1973

Haak, Bob. *Rembrandt Drawings.* 1976

Slive, Seymour. *Drawings of Rembrandt, with a Selection of Drawings by his Pupils and Followers,* 2 vols. 1965

White, Christopher. *The Drawings of Rembrandt.* 1962

ETCHINGS

Boon, K. G. *Rembrandt: The Complete Etchings.* 1963

Münz, Ludwig. *Rembrandt's Etchings,* 2 vols. 1952

White, Christopher. *Rembrandt as an Etcher: A Study of the Artist at Work,* 2 vols. 1969

—, and K. G. Boon. *Rembrandt's Etchings: An Illustrated Critical Catalogue,* 2 vols. 1969

LIST OF ILLUSTRATIONS

The following abbreviations have been used: *a* above; *b* below; *c* centre; *l* left; *r* right; Bibl. Nat. Bibliothèque Nationale.

COVER

Front *Self-portrait.* 1629. Oil on wood, 18 x 14 cm. Alte Pinakothek, Munich
Spine *The Conspiracy of Julius Civilis* (detail). 1661. Oil on canvas, 196 x 309 cm. Nationalmuseum, Stockholm
Back Figure of officer (detail). 1637. Painting, 62.5 x 47 cm. Mauritshuis, The Hague

OPENING

1 *The Company of Captain Frans Banning Cocq,* also known as *The Night Watch.* Watercolour copy. Album of Captain Cocq. Rijksmuseum, Amsterdam
2–9 *The Company of Captain Frans Banning Cocq,* known as *The Night Watch* (details). Oil on canvas, 359 x 438 cm. Rijksmuseum, Amsterdam
11 *Self-portrait in a Cap, Open-mouthed and Staring.* 1630. Etching. Bibl. Nat., Paris

CHAPTER 1

12 Attribution disputed. *The Mill. c.* 1650. Oil on canvas, 87.5 x 105.5 cm. Widener Collection, National Gallery of Art, Washington
13 *Rembrandt's Father with a Chain.* 1630. Etching. Bibl. Nat., Paris
14*a Rembrandt's Mother Seated, in Oriental Headdress.* 1631. Etching. Bibl. Nat., Paris
14*b* Pieter Bast. *View of Leiden* (detail). 1601. Engraving. Bibl. Nat., Paris
15 G. Braun and F. Hogenburg. 16th-century map of Leiden in *Civitates orbis terrarum,* Cologne, 1572–98. Bibl. Nat., Paris
16 Master of the St Elizabeth Panels. *The St Elizabeth's Day Flood with Dordrecht in the Background.* Late 15th century. Oil on canvas. Rijksmuseum, Amsterdam
17 The quay of the Old Rhine. Detail of a 17th-century map of Leiden. Engraving. Bibl. Nat., Paris
18*a* Hendrick Avercamp. *Recreation on the Ice.* Painting. Private collection, Lausanne
18*b The Skater.* 1639. Etching. Bibl. Nat., Paris
19 Jan Steen. *The Meal.* 1639. Painting. Louvre, Paris
20*a* Adriaen Pietersz van de Venne. Allegory of the truce of 1609 between the Archduke of Austria,

Governor of the South Netherlands and the states of the North Netherlands (detail). 1616. Painting. Louvre, Paris

20*b* East India Company House. 17th-century engraving. Bibl. Nat., Paris

21 Preserving herrings. Decoration of a Delft china plate. Haags Gemeentemuseum, The Hague

22–3 Ludolf Backhuysen. *The Dutch Fleet of the East India Company.* Painting. Louvre, Paris

24*a* Frans Hals. *Paulus van Beresteyn* (detail). Painting. Louvre, Paris

24*b* Frontispiece of the first edition of the Statenbijbel. Printed in Leiden in 1637. Bibl. Nat., Paris

25*a* Jacob van Swanenburgh. Interior of the library of the university of Leiden. Engraving. Bibl. Nat., Paris

25*b* Jacob van Swanenburgh. Anatomy theatre of the university of Leiden in 1610. Engraving in Frederik Muller, *Atlas.* Bibl. Nat., Paris

26 *The Angel and the Prophet Balaam* or *Balaam and the Ass.* 1626. Oil on canvas, 63 x 46.5 cm. Musée Cognac Jay, Paris

27*a* Pieter Lastman. *The Entombment.* Painting. Musée des Beaux Arts, Lille

27*b* Pieter Lastman. *The Angel and the Prophet Balaam.* 1622. Painting. Richard L. Feigen and Co., New York

28*a* Jan Lievens. *Self-portrait* (detail). *c.* 1635. Painting. Present whereabouts unknown. Photo courtesy Noortman & Brod, London

28–29 Salomon van Ruysdael. *The Ferry* (detail). Louvre, Paris

29*l* *The Stoning of St Stephen.* 1625. Oil on wood, 89.5 x 123.6 cm. Musée des Beaux Arts, Lyons

29*r* Pieter Jansz Saenredam. *The Cathedral of St Bavo in Haarlem* (detail). Louvre, Paris

30*a* *Old Man with a White Beard.* 1626. Oil on wood, 24 x 20.5 cm. Van der Bergh Collection, Wassenaar, Holland

30*b* *The Clemency of Titus.* 1626. Oil on wood, 90 x 122 cm. De Lakenhal Museum, Leiden

31 *Christ Driving the Moneychangers from the Temple.* 1626. Painting, 43 x 33 cm. Pushkin Museum, Moscow

32 and 33 (details) *Anna Accused by Tobit of Stealing the Kid.* 1626. Oil on wood, 39.5 x 30 cm. Rijksmuseum, Amsterdam

34*bl* *Rembrandt's Mother: Head.* 1628. Etching. Bibl. Nat., Paris

34*br* *Beggar in High Cap, Leaning on a Stick.* 1629. Etching. Bibl. Nat., Paris

34–5 *The Artist in his Studio. c.* 1628. Oil on wood, 24.8 x 31.7 cm. Museum of Fine Arts, Boston

35*cr* *Beggar with a Crippled Hand, Leaning on a Stick.* 1629. Etching. Bibl. Nat., Paris

35*b* Jacques Callot. *Beggar with a Crutch* in *Les Gueux.* Bibl. Nat., Paris

36*a* Jan Lievens. *Constantijn Huygens* (detail). *c.* 1626. Oil on wood. Rijksmuseum, Amsterdam

36*b* Preliminary drawing for *Judas Returning the Thirty Pieces of Silver. c.* 1629. Ecole Nationale Supérieure des Beaux Arts, Paris

36–7 *Judas Returning the Thirty Pieces of Silver.* 1629. Oil on wood, 80 x 102 cm. Private collection

38 *The Prophetess Anna.* 1631. Painting, 59.8 x 47.7 cm. Rijksmuseum, Amsterdam

39 Gerrit Dou. *An Old Woman* or *Rembrandt's Mother.* Painting. Louvre, Paris

CHAPTER 2

40 Jan van der Heyden. *The Herrengracht in Amsterdam* (detail). Painting. Louvre, Paris

41 *View of Amsterdam.* 1641. Etching. Bibl. Nat., Paris

42*l* After Frans Hals. Portrait of René Descartes. Painting. Louvre, Paris

42*ar, acr, b* Rembrandt's signatures, dating from 1627, 1631 and 1632 respectively

43 Emanuel de Witte. *The Courtyard of the Old Exchange, Amsterdam* (detail). 1653. Oil on wood, 49 x 47.5 cm. Willem van der Vorm Foundation, Boymans-van Beuningen Museum, Rotterdam

44–5 *Scholar in a Room with a Winding Stair* or *The Philosopher.* 1631. Painting, 29 x 33 cm. Louvre, Paris

46*a* Thomas de Keyser. *The Anatomy Lesson of Dr Sebastian Egbertsz.* 1619. Painting. Historisch Museum, Amsterdam

46*b* Pieter Michelsz van Miereveld. *Anatomy Lesson of Dr van der Meer in Delft.* Painting. Gemeentemusea, Delft

46–7 *The Anatomy Lesson of Professor Tulp.* 1632. Oil on canvas, 162.5 x 216.5. Mauritshuis, The Hague

48–9 *Ibid.* (details)

50 *Saskia in a Straw Hat.* 1633. Silverpoint on vellum, 18.5 x 10.7 cm. Kupferstichkabinett, Staatliche Museen, Berlin

51 *Saskia Smiling with a Plumed Beret.* 1633. Painting, 52.5 x 44.5 cm. Gemäldegalerie, Staatliche Kunstsammlungen, Dresden

52*l* *The Raising of the Cross.* 1634. Oil on canvas, 95.6 x 72.2 cm. Alte Pinakothek, Munich

52*r* *The Descent from the Cross* (detail). 1634. Oil on canvas, 89 x 65 cm. Alte Pinakothek, Munich

53 *The Entombment. c.* 1639. Oil on wood, 32 x 40.5 cm. Glasgow University Art Collection

54 *The Blinding of Samson.* 1636. Oil on canvas, 236 x 302 cm. Städelsches Kunstinstitut, Frankfurt

54–5 Ferdinand Bol. *Mother Nursing her Child.* Drawing. Louvre, Paris

55*a* Attribution uncertain. *The Studio.* Drawing. Louvre, Paris

55cr *The Pancake Woman*. 1635. Etching. Bibl. Nat., Paris

56–7 *Artemisia Receiving the Ashes of Mausolus* or *Sophonisba Receiving the Poisoned Cup*. 1634. Prado, Madrid

57 *Self-portrait with Saskia*. 1636. Etching. Bibl. Nat., Paris

58 *Saskia as Flora*. 1634. Oil on canvas, 125 x 101 cm. State Hermitage Museum, St Petersburg

59 *Portrait of Saskia van Ulenborch* (detail). 1634. Painting, 99.5 x 78.5 cm. Staatliche Kunstsammlungen, Kassel

60 *Self-portrait with Saskia*. 1636. Oil on canvas, 161 x 131 cm. Staatliche Kunstsammlungen, Dresden

61a *Jan Uytenbogaert, the Receiver-General* or *The Goldweigher*. 1639. Etching. Bibl. Nat., Paris

61b *Two Men Standing in Oriental Dress*. Drawing. Louvre, Paris

62 *The House in Sint Anthoniesbreestraat*. Engraving. Het Rembrandthuis, Amsterdam

62–3 After Raphael's *Portrait of Baldassare Castiglione*. 1639. Drawing. Graphische Sammlung Albertina, Vienna

63ar Raphael. *Portrait of Baldassare Castiglione*. 1516. Louvre, Paris

64 *Self-portrait in Working Dress*. c. 1654. Het Rembrandthuis, Amsterdam

65 Attribution disputed. *The Flayed Ox*. 1640

66l *Portrait of Cornelis Claesz Anslo*. 1640. Drawing. Rothschild Collection, Louvre, Paris

66–7 *Portrait of Cornelis Claesz Anslo with a Woman*. 1641. Painting, 176 x 210 cm. Staatliche Museen, Berlin

67b *Cornelis Claesz Anslo, Mennonite Preacher*. 1641. Etching. Bibl. Nat., Paris

68–9 *Landscape with a Stone Bridge*. 1637. Oil on wood, 29.5 x 42.5 cm. Rijksmuseum, Amsterdam

70 *Portrait of Nicolaes Bruyningh*. 1652. Oil on canvas, 105 x 90 cm. Staatliche Kunstsammlungen, Kassel

71 *The Artist Drawing from a Model*. 1639. Etching. Bibl. Nat., Paris

72 Bartholomeus van der Helst. *The Governors of the Honourable Archers' Guild in Amsterdam* (detail). 1653. Painting. Louvre, Paris

73l *Saskia Ill, with Large White Headdress*. 1641. Etching. Bibl. Nat., Paris

73r *Saskia Lying Ill in Bed* (detail). 1638. Etching. Bibl. Nat., Paris

74–5 Cornelis Dankerts. Map of Amsterdam in 1662. City Archives, Amsterdam

76 *Saskia Lying Ill in Bed* (detail). 1638. Etching. Bibl. Nat., Paris

77a *The Company of Captain Frans Banning Cocq* or *The Night Watch*. 1642. Oil on canvas, 359 x 438 cm. Rijksmuseum, Amsterdam

77b *The Sick Man of Samaria*. c. 1650. Drawing. Louvre, Paris

CHAPTER 3

78 *The Company of Captain Frans Banning Cocq* or *The Night Watch* (detail). 1642. Oil on canvas, 359 x 438 cm. Rijksmuseum, Amsterdam

79 Samuel van Hoogstraten. *The Slippers*. Painting. Louvre, Paris

80b Geertge Dircx. c. 1642. Drawing. Teylers Museum, Haarlem

80–1 *The Three Trees*. 1643. Etching. Bibl. Nat., Paris

81ar *Ibid*. (detail)

81b *Het Ledekant* or *Le Lit à la française*. 1646. Etching. Bibl. Nat., Paris

82 *St Jerome beside a Pollard Willow*. 1648. Etching. Bibl. Nat., Paris

83a *Christ at Emmaus*. 1648. Oil on wood, 68 x 65 cm. Louvre, Paris

83b *The Holy Family with the Curtain*. 1646. Painting, 46.5 x 48.5 cm. Staatliche Kunstsammlungen, Kassel

84 *The Artist's Son Titus*. c. 1650. Painting, 62 x 52 cm. Norton Simon Foundation, Pasadena, California

85 *Portrait of Geertge Dircx*. c. 1642. Drawing. British Museum, London

86 *The Sleeping Nymph and a Satyr*. Drawing. Louvre, Paris

87 Hendrickje Stoffels. 1654. Painting, 74 x 61 cm. Louvre, Paris

88a *The Shell*. 1650. Etching. Bibl. Nat., Paris

88–9 *Six's Bridge*. 1645. Etching. Bibl. Nat., Paris

89a *Jan Six at his Desk*. 1655. Drawing. Louvre, Paris

90b *The Woman Taken in Adultery*. Drawing. Louvre, Paris

90–1 *The Three Crosses* (1st version). 1653. Etching. Bibl. Nat., Paris

91r *The Three Crosses* (4th version). 1653. Etching. Bibl. Nat., Paris

92l Attribution disputed. *The Polish Rider*. 1655. Painting, 115 x 135.5 cm. Frick Collection, New York

92r *Woman Looking out of the Window*. c. 1655. Rothschild Bequest, Louvre, Paris

93 *Bathsheba*. 1654. Painting, 142 x 142 cm. Louvre, Paris

94 *A Woman Bathing in a Stream*. 1654. Painting, 61.8 x 47 cm. National Gallery, London

95 *Hendrickje at the Window*. 1656–7. Painting, 86 x 65 cm. Staatliche Museen, Berlin

96 *Titus at his Desk*. 1655. Oil on canvas, 77 x 63 cm. Boymans-van Beuningen Museum, Rotterdam

96–7 *The Unjust Steward*. Drawing. Louvre, Paris

97ar Titian. Two studies for *The Death of St Peter Martyr*. Louvre, Paris

98 Notice advertising the sale of Rembrandt's possessions in 1658. British Museum, London

99*a* Andrea Mantegna. *Dead Christ*. Painting. Pinacoteca di Brera, Milan

99*b* *The Anatomy Lesson of Dr Johannes Deyman*. 1656. Oil on canvas, 100 x 134 cm. Rijksmuseum, Amsterdam

CHAPTER 4

100 *Self-portrait holding his Palette, Brushes and Maulstick*. c. 1663. Oil on canvas, 114.3 x 94 cm. Iveagh Bequest, Kenwood House

101 *Titus Reading*. 1656–7. Oil on canvas, 112 x 81.5 cm. Kunsthistorisches Museum, Vienna

102*l* *Self-portrait, Leaning Forward, as if Listening*. 1628. Etching. Bibl. Nat., Paris

102*c* *Self-portrait with a Broad Nose*. 1628. Etching. Bibl. Nat., Paris

102*r* *Self-portrait in Fur Cap and Light Dress*. 1630. Etching. Bibl. Nat., Paris

103*al* *Self-portrait Angry*. 1630. Etching. Bibl. Nat., Paris

103*ac* *Self-portrait Open-mouthed, as if Shouting*. 1630. Etching. Bibl. Nat., Paris

103*ar* *Self-portrait in a Soft Cap*. 1634. Etching. Bibl. Nat., Paris

103*b* *Self-portrait*. 1658. Oil on canvas, 129 x 101 cm. Frick Collection, New York

104*l* *Self-portrait* (detail). 1629. Oil on wood, 37 x 29 cm. Mauritshuis, The Hague

104–5 *Self-portrait*. 1634. Painting, 67 x 54 cm. Uffizi, Florence

105*r* *Self-portrait* (detail). 1629. Oil on wood, 37 x 29 cm. Mauritshuis, The Hague

106–7 (detail) and 107 *Self-portrait*. 1640. Oil on canvas, 89.9 x 74.9 cm. National Gallery, London

108*l* *Self-portrait* (detail). 1660. Oil on canvas, 111 x 90 cm. Louvre, Paris

108–9 *Self-portrait* (detail). 1669. Oil on canvas, 86 x 70.5 cm. National Gallery, London

109*c* *Self-portrait* (detail). 1669. Oil on canvas, 59 x 51 cm. Mauritshuis, The Hague

109*r* The three preceding self-portraits

110*a* *Jan Six*. 1647. Etching. Bibl. Nat., Paris

110*b* *The Keizerskroon Inn in the Calverstraat*. Coloured drawing. City Archives, Amsterdam

111 *Titus in Friar's Habit*. 1660. Oil on canvas, 85 x 78 cm. Rijksmuseum, Amsterdam

112–3*a* *The Conspiracy of Julius Civilis*. 1661. Oil on canvas, 196 x 309 cm. Nationalmuseum, Stockholm

112–3*b* *Ibid*. (detail)

113*br* Preparatory drawing for *The Conspiracy of Julius Civilis*. Staatliche Graphische Sammlung, Munich

114 *Juno*. 1664–5. Oil on canvas, 127 x 107.3 cm. Armand Hammer Collection, Los Angeles

115 *Ibid*. (detail)

116 Ferdinand Bol. *The Guild of Wine Merchants*. Painting. Alte Pinakothek, Munich

116–7 *The Portrait of the Syndics of the Clothmakers' Guild*. 1662. Oil on canvas, 191 x 279 cm. Rijksmuseum, Amsterdam

117*b* Study for *The Syndics*. c. 1662. Drawing. Boymans-van Beuningen Museum, Rotterdam

118 *Aristotle Contemplating the Bust of Homer*. 1653. Oil on canvas, 143.5 x 136.5 cm. Metropolitan Museum of Art, New York

119 *Alexander the Great*. 1663. Painting, 118 x 91 cm. Fundaçao Calouste Gulbenkian, Lisbon

121 *Frederick Rihel on Horseback*. 1663. Oil on canvas, 294.5 x 241 cm. National Gallery, London

122*l* Raphael. *Self-portrait*. Uffizi, Florence

122*r* Rubens. *Self-portrait*. Uffizi, Florence

123*l* Velazquez. *Self-portrait*. Uffizi, Florence

123*r* *Self-portrait*. 1664. Oil on canvas, 71 x 57 cm. Uffizi, Florence

124 Drawing for composition of *The Jewish Bride*. c. 1668. Private collection, Berlin

124–5 *The Jewish Bride* or *The Bridal Couple*. c. 1668. Oil on canvas, 121.5 x 166.5 cm. Rijksmuseum, Amsterdam

126 *A Family Group*. 1669. Oil on canvas, 126 x 167 cm. Staatliches Herzog Anton Ulrich Museum, Braunschweig, Germany

126–7 *The Ruin*. 1650. Painting, 67 x 87.5 cm. Staatliche Kunstsammlungen

127*ar* *Westerkerk*. Drawing. Private collection, Rotterdam

128 *Self-portrait*. 1665. Oil on canvas, 82.5 x 65 cm. Wallraf Richartz Museum, Cologne

DOCUMENTS

129 *Art Student Drawing from a Cast*. c. 1641. Etching. Bibl. Nat., Paris

130 Rembrandt's house in the Sint Anthoniesbreestraat, Amsterdam. Photograph

136 *Judas Returning the Thirty Pieces of Silver* (detail). 1629. Oil on wood, 80 x 102 cm. Private collection

138 Cornelis de Brellieur. *Interior of a Gallery of Pictures and 'Objets d'art'*. Painting, 935 x 1230 cm. Louvre, Paris

139 *The Storm on the Sea of Galilee*. 1633. Oil on canvas. Isabella Stewart Gardner Museum, Boston

140 *The Entombment*. 1654. Etching. Bibl. Nat., Paris

141 *The Jewish Bride* (detail). c. 1668. Oil on canvas, 121.5 x 166.5 cm. Rijksmuseum, Amsterdam

142 *Saskia as Flora*. 1635. Oil on canvas, 121 x 96 cm. National Gallery, London

143 *David in Prayer*. 1652. Etching. Bibl. Nat., Paris

144 *The Company of Captain Frans Banning Cocq*

or *The Night Watch.* 1642. Oil on canvas, 359 x 438 cm. Rijksmuseum, Amsterdam
147 *Ibid.* (detail)
148 *Ibid.* 1650. Watercolour copy. Album of Captain Cocq. 1650. Rijksmuseum, Amsterdam
149 *Ibid.* (detail). Oil on canvas, 359 x 438 cm. Rijksmuseum, Amsterdam
150 *Jan Cornelisz Sylvius, Preacher: Posthumous Portrait.* 1646. Etching. Bibl. Nat., Paris
151 *Faust in his Study.* 1652. Etching. Bibl. Nat., Paris
152 *The Blindness of Tobit* (detail). 1651. Etching. Bibl. Nat., Paris
153 *The Emperor Timur on the Throne. c.* 1635. After an Indian miniature. Pen and ink with wash on paper, 186 x 187 cm. Louvre, Paris
154 *Beggar Seated on a Bank.* 1630. Etching. Bibl. Nat., Paris
156 *Adam and Eve* (detail). 1638. Etching. Bibl. Nat., Paris
157 Abraham Furnerius. *View of the Bridge at Grimnesse-sluis in Amsterdam.* Louvre, Paris
158 *Abraham's Sacrifice.* 1636. Alte Pinakothek, Munich
159 *Self-portrait. c.* 1627–8. Pen and brush, brown and grey ink. 12.7 x 9.5 cm. British Museum, London
161 *Birds of Paradise.* Pen and brown wash with white gouache. Louvre, Paris
162*l* Attribution disputed. *Bust of an Old Woman.* Oil on wood, 35 x 29 cm. C. 42. Von Bohle Collection, Essen
162*r* Attribution disputed. Etching. B. 353. Bibl. Nat., Paris
163*l* *Rembrandt's Mother: Head.* 1628. B. 352. Rijksmuseum, Amsterdam
163*r* *Rembrandt's Mother: Bust.* 1628. B. 354. British Museum, London
165 *Aristotle Contemplating the Bust of Homer.* 1653. Oil on canvas, 143.5 x 136.5 cm. Metropolitan Museum of Art, New York
166 Anonymous. *View of Sint Anthoniespoort in Amsterdam.* Drawing. Louvre, Paris
167 *Self-portrait.* 1652. Oil on canvas, 112 x 81.5 cm. Kunsthistorisches Museum, Vienna

INDEX

Figures in italic refer to pages on which captions appear.

A

Abraham's Sacrifice 158
Adam and Eve 156
Adoration of the Shepherds, The 82
Album amicorum (Jan Six) 89
Alexander the Great 117, 118
Amsterdam 21, *26*, 28, 39, 42, 43, *43*, 48, 49, 62, 63, 89, 90, 98, *107*, 112, 115, 116, 117, 120, *120*, *123*, 152, 155, 156, 164, 165, 166; map of *75*; view of *41*
Anatomy Lesson of: Dr Johannes Deyman, The 98, *99*, 141; Dr Sebastian Egbertsz, The (Thomas de Keyser) 46; Dr van der Meer, The (Pieter van Miereveld) *46*;

Professor Tulp, The *47*, 48, *48*, 98
Angel and the Prophet Balaam, The (Pieter Lastman) 26
Anna Accused by Tobit of Stealing the Kid 30, *33*, 82
Anslo, Cornelis Claesz 66, 67, *67*
Ariosto, Portrait of (Titian) 63, 64, *107*
Aristotle Contemplating the Bust of Homer 92, 118, *118*, 164–7, *165*
Artemisia Receiving the Ashes of Mausolus (or Sophonisba Receiving the Poisoned Cup) 57
Artist Drawing from a Model, The *71*
Artist in his Studio, The 34, *35*
Artist's Son Titus, The 84
Art Student Drawing from a Cast 129

B

Backer, Jacob Adriaensz 54, 73, 80
Balaam and the Ass (or

The Angel and the Prophet Balaam) 26, 63, 65
Baldassare Castiglione, Portrait of (Raphael) 62, 63, 64, *107*
Baldinucci, Filippo 76, 82, 84, 137
Bathsheba 93
Becker, Harmen *115*, 120
Beggar in High Cap, Leaning on a Stick 34
Beggar Seated on a Bank 154
Beggar with a Crippled Hand, Leaning on a Stick 35
Beggar with a Crutch (Jacques Callot) 35
Belten, Pieter 62
Birds of Paradise 161
Blanchem, Reijmptje van (Rembrandt's maternal grandmother) 14, 17
Blinding of Samson, The 54
Blindness of Tobit, The 152
Bol, Ferdinand 54, *55*, 80, *116*, 134
Bruyningh, Nicolaes,

Portrait of 71
Buchell, Aernout van 29, 30, 34
Bust of an Old Woman (attribution disputed) 162

C

Callot, Jacques 35, *35*, 65, 97, 134
Caravaggio 26, *27*
Cathedral of St Bavo in Haarlem, The (Pieter Saenredam) 29
Charles V (Titian) 120
chiaroscuro *27*, 71–2, *71*, 148–9, 156
Christ at Emmaus 83
Christ Driving the Moneychangers from the Temple 30, *30*
Circumcision, The 34, 82
Clark, Kenneth 159
Claudel, Paul 150–2
Clemency of Titus, The 30
Cocq, Captain Frans Banning 72–3, *72*, *75*; see Company of Company of: Captain Bas, The (Govaert

Flinck) 73; *Captain Cornelis Bicker, The* (Joachim von Sandrart) 73; *Captain Roelof Bicker, The* (Bartholomeus van der Helst) 73; *Captain Frans Banning Cocq, The* (or *The Night Watch*) 1, 2–9, 73, 76, *76*, 77, *77*, 79, *79*, 110, 144–9, *144*, *147*, *148*, *149*, 152; *Captain De Graeff, The* (Jacob Adriaensz Backer) 73; *Captain van Vlooswijck, The* (Nicolaes Eliasz Pickenoy) 73 *Conspiracy of Julius Civilis, The* 112, *113*, 115, 116 *Courtyard of the Old Exchange, Amsterdam, The* (Emanuel de Witte) *43*

D

David in Prayer 143
David Presenting the Head of Goliath to Saul 30
Dead Christ (Andrea Mantegna) 98, *99*
Death of St Peter Martyr, The (Titian) *96*
Death of the Virgin, The 73
Decker, Jeremias de 101, 124
Delacroix, Eugène 138–40, 141
Descartes, René 36, 41, 42, *42*
Descent from the Cross, The 52, 53
Description of the Town of Leiden (Johannes Orlers) 65
Deyman, Dr Johannes 98, *98*, *99*; see *Anatomy Lesson of Dircx, Geertge* 80, *80*, 85, *85*
Dou, Gerrit 38, *39*

Dürer, Albrecht *35*, 134
Dutch East India Company 21, *23*
Dutch Fleet of the East India Company (Ludolf Backhuysen) *23*

E

East India Company House *21*
Eekhout, Gerbrand van den 54
Emperor Timour on the Throne, The 153
Entombment, The 52, *53*, 140
Entombment (Pieter Lastman) 27

F

Family Group, A 126
Faure, Elie 156–7
Faust in his Study 151
Ferry, The (Salomon van Ruysdael) 28
Flayed Ox, The (attribution disputed) 65
Flight into Egypt, The 30, 34
Flinck, Govaert 54, 73, 80, 97, 112
Fromentin, Eugène 144–9, 152

G

Gelder, Aert de 112
Genet, Jean 153–5
Gogh, Vincent van 140–3
Governors of the Honourable Archers' Guild in Amsterdam, The (Bartholomeus van der Helst) 72
Guild of St Luke 111
Guild of Wine Merchants, The (Ferdinand Bol) *116*

H

Hals, Frans 21, *24*, *42*, 134, 141, 142, 143,

147, 153, 154
Hazlitt, William 158
Heertsbeeck, Isaac van 90, 120
Heller, Joseph 164–7
Helst, Bartholomeus van der *72*, 73
Hendrickje at the Window 93
Herrengracht in Amsterdam, The (Jan van der Heyden) *41*
Holbein, Hans, the Younger 120
Holy Family with the Curtain, The 82, *83*
Hoogstraten, Samuel van 34, 79, *79*, 163
Houbraken, Arnold 38, 81, 82, 84, 115, 123, 125
House in Sint Anthoniesbreestraat, The 62, *130*
Huygens, Constantijn 36, *36*, 37, *37*, 38, 52, *54*, 61, 124, 136–7

I

Inventory of Rembrandt's property 96–7, *96*, 130–5

J

Jaegher, Hendrickje Stoffelsdochter see Stoffels, Hendrickje
Jewish Bride, The (or *The Bridal Couple*) 124, *124*, 141, *141*
Joseph's Dream 82
Judas Returning the Thirty Pieces of Silver 37, *37*, 136
Juno 115, 120
Jupiter and Antiope (Titian) 86

K

Keil, Bernhardt 137
Keizerskroon Inn 75, 98, 99, 110, *110*
Ker, Robert (Earl of

Ancrum) 38
Kloveniersdoelen 73, 76
Koninck, Philips 110
Kretzer, Marten 86

L

Landscape with a Stone Bridge 69
Lastman, Pieter 26, *26*, 27, *27*, 28, *75*, 97, 131, 132, 134
Last Supper, The (Leonardo da Vinci) 55
Leiden 13, 14, *14*, 18, 24, *24*, 26, *26*, 27, 28, 29, *34*, *38*, 39, 42, *42*, 43, 64, 93, 159, 166; plan and view of *14*, *17*; university 24, *25*, 89
Lievens, Jan 28, *28*, 36, *36*, 37, 38, 97, 130
Lit à la Française, Le (or *Het Ledekant*) 81
Loo, Jan van 110, 124
Loo, Magdalena van (wife of Titus van Rijn) *75*, 123, 126
Lopez, Alphonso 62, 63, 65, *107*
Ludick, Lodewijk van 90, 110, 120

M

Man with the Golden Helmet, The (attribution disputed) 92
Meal, The (Jan Steen) 18
Medici, Cosimo III de' 120, 122, *122*, 123
Medici, Leopoldo de' 122, *122*
Michelangelo Buonarroti 43, 97, 133
Mill, The 13
Mother Nursing her Child (Ferdinand Bol) 55
Musical Gathering, A 102
Music Party, The 30

N

Night Watch, The see
*Company of Captain
Frans Banning Cocq,
The*

O

*Old Man with a White
Beard 30*
Old Woman, An (Gerrit
Dou) *39*
Orlers, Johannes 13, 25,
26, 39, 65
Oudekerk 77, 91, 118

P

*Pancake Woman, The
55*
Paulus van Beresteyn
(Frans Hals) *24*
Pickenoy, Nicolaes
Eliasz 73
Polish Rider, The
(attribution disputed)
92, 120
*Presentation of Christ in
the Temple, The 39*
*Prophetess Anna, The 38,
39*

R

*Raising of the Cross, The
52–3, 52*
Raphael 43, 62, 63, *63,*
96, 97, 102, *107,
122,* 131, 132, 133,
138
Recreation On the Ice
(Hendrick Avercamp)
18
Rembrandt Research
Project 160–3
*Rembrandt's Mother:
Bust 163*
*Rembrandt's Mother:
Head 34, 163*
*Rest on the Flight into
Egypt, The* 34
*Return of the Prodigal
Son, The* 155
Rihel, Frederick 120,
120
Rijn Adriaen van (2nd

brother) 17
Rijn, Cornelia van (1st
daughter, born and
died 1638) 64; (2nd
daughter, born and
died 1640) 64; (3rd
daughter, born 1654
to Hendrickje) 91,
118, 126
Rijn, Cornelis van (3rd
brother) 17
Rijn, Gerrit van (eldest
brother) 17
Rijn, Harmen van
(father) 13, *13,* 14,
17, 18, 39, 43
Rijn, Lijsbeth van
(younger sister) 17
Rijn, Machteld van
(elder sister) 17
Rijn, Rumbartus van
(1st son, born 1635
and died 1636) 54
Rijn, Titia van
(granddaughter, born
1669 to Titus and
Magdalena van Loo)
126
Rijn, Titus van (4th
child, 1641–68) 72,
75, 76, 77, 80, *80,
84,* 85, *85,* 93, 110,
111, 120, 123, 126,
127, 134, 154, 155,
167; *at his Desk 96;
in Friar's Habit 111;
Reading 101*
Rijn, Willem van (4th
brother) 17
Rubens, Peter Paul 38,
86, 97, 110, *122,*
133, 139, 147
Ruffo, Don Antonio
90, 117, 118, 165
Ruin, The 126

S

*St Elizabeth's Day Flood
with Dordrecht in the
Background, The*
(Master of the St
Elizabeth Panels) 17
*St Jerome beside a
Pollard Willow 82*
*St John the Baptist
Preaching* 90
St Paul in Prison 30

*St Peter's Denial of
Christ* 30
Samson and Delilah 30
Sandrart, Joachim von
24, 73
Saskia see Ulenborch,
Saskia van
*Scholar in a Room with a
Winding Stair* (or *The
Philospher*) *45*
Schooten, Joris van 28
Seghers, Hercules 35,
97, 130, 131, 132,
134
*Self-portraits 11, 63, 64,
101,* 102–3, *102,
103, 105, 107, 109,*
110, 122, *123, 126,
154, 159, 167; with
Saskia 57, 60*
Self-portrait (Jan
Lievens) 28
Self-portrait (Raphael)
122
Self-portrait (Rubens)
122
Self-portrait (Velazquez)
123
Shell, The 88
*Sick Man of Samaria,
The 77*
*Simeon and the Child
Jesus in the Temple*
126
Six, Jan *75,* 89, 90, 97,
110, *110,* 120, 134;
*at his Desk 89; Six's
Bridge 89*
Skater, The 18
Skeleton Rider, The 120
*Sleeping Nymph and a
Satyr, The 86*
Slippers, The (Samuel
van Hoogstraten) *79*
Stadholder 20, 28, 36,
38, 52, *52, 53, 54,*
61, 62, 82, 136
Statenbijbel (State
Bible) *24,* 25
Stoffels, Hendrickje 85,
86, *86,* 90, 91, *92,
93,* 111, 118, 126,
127, 154, 155, 167
*Stoning of St Stephen,
The* 29, *29*
*Storm on the Sea of
Galilee, The 139*
Studio, The (attribution

uncertain) *55*
Suydtbroek, Cornelia
'Neeltge' van
(Rembrandt's
mother) 13, 14, *14,*
17, *34, 39,* 64, *163*
Swanenburgh, Jacob
van *25,* 26
Sylvius, Jan Cornelisz
50, 66, 67, 88, *150*
*Syndics of the
Clothmakers' Guild,
The Portrait of the*
115–6, *116,* 141

T

Thijsz, Christoffel 62,
90, 92
Three Crosses, The 91
Three Trees, The 81, *81*
Titian 43, 63, 64, 86,
86, 96, 97, 98, 102,
107, 120, 133, 139,
147
Titus, see Rijn, Titus
van
Tulp, Professor
Nicolaas Pieterszoon
46, 47, *47,* 48, *48,
75,* 97; see *Anatomy
Lesson of*
Twelve Year Truce 20;
allegory of (Adriaen
van de Venne) *20*
*Two Men Standing in
Oriental Dress* 61
Two Scholars Disputing
30

U

Ulenborch, Hendrick
van 43, 50, 54, 62
Ulenborch, Saskia van
(born 1612, married
Rembrandt 1634,
died 1642) 49, 50,
50, 54, 55, *57, 59,
60,* 61, 62, 72, 73,
73, 75, 76–7, 80, 85,
86, *86,* 91, 110, 118,
166, 167; *as Flora 59,
142,* 153; *Ill, with
Large White Headdress
73; in a Straw Hat
50; Lying Ill in Bed
73, 77; Portrait of*

Saskia in a Red Hat 90; *Portrait of Saskia van Ulenborch* 59; *Self-portrait with Saskia* 57, 60; *Smiling with a Plumed Beret* 50
Ulenborch, Titia van 65
Unjust Steward, The 96
Uytenbogaert, Jan (preacher) 66, 67

Uytenbogaert, Jan, *The Receiver-General* (or *The Goldweigher*) 61

V

Velazquez 38, *123*, 147
View of the Bridge at Grimnesse-sluis in Amsterdam (Abraham Furnerius) *157*

W

Westerkerk 42, *75*, 118, 126, *126*
Witsen, Cornelis 90
Woman Bathing in a Stream, A 93
Woman Looking out of the Window 92
Woman Taken in Adultery, The 82, *91*

Y

Youth Surprised by Death 73

Z

Zeuxis 102, 124

PHOTO CREDITS

ACKNOWLEDGMENTS

Grateful acknowledgment is made for permission to use material from the following works:
(pp. 164–7) Joseph Heller, *Picture This*, reprinted by permission of The Putnam Publishing Group, New York, copyright © 1988 by Joseph Heller; (pp. 160–3) *A Corpus of Rembrandt Paintings*, Vol. 1, reprinted by permission of the Rembrandt Research Project, Amsterdam, and Kluwer Academic Publishers, Dordrecht, 1982; (pp. 52–3, 61–2, 130–5) Walter L. Strauss and Marjon van der Meulen (eds.), *The Rembrandt Documents*, pp. 129, 167, 173, 349–87, reprinted by permission of Abaris Books, Inc., Pleasantville, New York, USA, 1979; (pp. 140–3) *The Complete Letters of Vincent van Gogh*, trans. by J. van Goch-Bonger and C. de Dood, by permission of Thames and Hudson Ltd, London, and Little, Brown and Company, Boston, Massachusetts, USA, in conjunction with The New York Graphic Society, all rights reserved, 1958.

Pascal Bonafoux
is an art historian and author
whose works include *Rembrandt, autoportrait*,
winner in 1985 of the Académie Française's Prix
Charles-Blanc and the Prix Elie Faure et Gutenberg;
Van Gogh par Vincent (1986);
and the novels *Annonce Classée* (1985);
and *Blessé grave* (1987).
He is the author of *Van Gogh:
The Passionate Eye*
in the New Horizons series.

© Gallimard 1990
English translation © Thames and Hudson Ltd, London,
and Harry N. Abrams, Inc., New York, 1992

Translated by Alexandra Campbell

Printed and bound in Italy by
Editoriale Libraria, Trieste